THEORY OF LEGAL PRINCIPLES

Law and Philosophy Library

VOLUME 81

THEORY OF LEGAL PRINCIPLES

By

HUMBERTO ÁVILA

Professor of Public Law at the
Federal University of Rio Grande do Sul, Brazil
Ph.D in Law (University of Munich, 2001)

Springer

A C.I.P. Catalogue record for this book is available from the Library of Congress.

ISBN 978-1-4020-5878-3 (HB)
ISBN 978-1-4020-5879-0 (e-book)

Published by Springer,
P.O. Box 17, 3300 AA Dordrecht, The Netherlands.

www.springer.com

Printed on acid-free paper

THE AUTHOR

HUMBERTO ÁVILA is a specialist in Corporate Finance from the School of Economic Sciences of the Federal University at Rio Grande do Sul (UFRGS), and a Master in Law from the Law School of UFRGS. His thesis "Provisional Measure in the 1988 Constitution" was published by Editora Sérgio Fabris in 1997. With a CNPq-granted scholarship, he went to the University of Munich, Germany in 1996, where he obtained a Certificate of Studies in Methodology of the Science of Law under the instruction of Claus-Wilhelm Canaris, and the degree of Doctor in Law under the instruction of Klaus Vogel. His *summa cum laude* doctorate dissertation was published in 2002 by Baden-Baden's Nomos, under the title "*Materiell verfassungsrechtliche Beschränkungen der Besteuerungsgewalt in der brasilianischen Verfassung und im deutschen Grundgesetz*" (Substantive constitutional limitations to the power to tax in the Brazilian Constitution and German Fundamental Law).

Besides practicing law and writing legal opinions in Porto Alegre, the author is also a Professor of Tax, Finance and Economic Law at the School of Law of UFRGS, where he was admitted through a public contest in which he qualified with the first place. He is a Professor of the LL.M and Ph.D. programs at UFRGS, where he is also a Member of the Graduate Program Coordinating Committee and the Coordinator of the Tax Law Specialization Program.

The author is the President and a Founding Member of the International Institute of Public Law Studies (IIEDE) and a counselor in the Consulting Board of the Brazilian Society of Public Law (SBDP). He is also a member of the Brazilian Institute of Tax Law (IBDT), the Brazilian Association of Finance Law (ABDF), the International Fiscal Association (IFA), the Lawyer Institute of Rio Grande do Sul (IARGS), the Institute of Tax Studies (IET/RS), the Luso-German Association of Jurisprudence and the Brazilian-German Association of Jurisprudence.

To Ana Paula, Geórgia and André, with love.

ACKNOWLEDGEMENTS

Every work, however short in length or large in ambition, depends on the support and encouragement of several people. So does this study. Thus, I wish and am pleased to thank:

— my wife Ana Paula, for her constant support to my academic efforts as well as for her critical and attentive reading of the original text of this study;

— my friend and Master José Souto Maior Borges, an impressive scholar who will not surrender his independence and convictions for easy and superficial success, for his initial and permanent encouragement;

— my dearest Geórgia and André, wonderful "little tots" that flood me with happiness, for giving sense to my efforts;

— Professors Almiro do Couto e Silva and Ricardo Lobo Torres, Masters by knowledge and not by force, examples of erudition, humanity and generosity, to whom the Brazilian edition was dedicated;

— Professor Eros Roberto Grau, for his general and generous support to my academic career;

— Professor Frederick Schauer, prestigious legal philosopher, for his generous welcome at Harvard University for my post-doctorate research and for the availability in directing its publication in English.

The original text of this work, initially written in Portuguese, was translated by Jorge Todeschini, whom I thank for the superb translation. A few marginal changes were made by the author and a few others were suggested by Professor Frederick Schauer.

FOREWORD TO THE GERMAN EDITION (THEORIE DER RECHTSPRINZIPIEN)

I.

In the past few decades, the most important forward thrust in the fields of Legal Theory and Philosophy has come mainly from the Anglo-American legal universe. That is especially true of the theme of general principles of Law, in which, following the works of *Ronald Dworkin*, the distinction between rules and principles made its way into the German-speaking legal universe, having found many followers despite some variations and developments in some aspects. The fact that this theme is intensely debated in the Ibero-American legal universe as well has not yet been presented enough in our country.

We are lucky, therefore, that Humberto Bergmann Ávila, with his profound knowledge of the German Legal Science and excellent command of the German language, has presented his "Theory of Legal Principles" also as a dissertation in German. Born in 1970, the author is a Professor of Tax, Finance, Economic and Constitutional Law at the Federal University at Rio Grande do Sul and a lawyer in Porto Alegre, Brazil. He is connected to the German Legal Science above all for his 2002 Doctor degree obtained with his dissertation on "Substantive Constitutional Limitations to the Power to Tax in the Brazilian Constitution and German Fundamental Law," which was presented to the Ludwig-Maximilians-Universität in Munich and published in Baden-Baden in 2002.

II.

Despite his openness to the positions developed heretofore and his willingness to incorporate and preserve fruitful viewpoints of other writers, the author imprints this current work with a clearly independent profile and original conception. An initial thesis of pivotal importance states that the opposition of rule and principle, both understood to the same extent as norms, cannot be seen as an exclusive contradiction. Rather, a legal norm can operate both as a rule and as a principle. Furthermore, the author does not acknowledge the specificity of principles in the fact that they can and ought to be balanced and have a dimension of weight; rather, he proves that this is fundamentally true of rules as well. Consequently he looks for the distinction between rules and principles somewhere else, and finds it firstly in the fact that rules have a direct description of a behavior or a jurisdiction assignment as its object, aiming only indirectly to the realization of a goal, whereas principles directly aim to the realization of a goal and only indirectly influence the behavior or jurisdiction assignments required to achieve such goals. Against that backdrop, the author furthers additional criteria and develops a different proposal of his own to distinguish between rules and principles.

Next, he expands his concept with an additional plane, adding postulates to the rules and principles. In doing so, he has in mind criteria such as proportionality, reasonableness, and legal efficiency and certainty, which are usually called principles, quite often without much thought. The author faces such use of language and such way of thinking by arguing that postulates, differently from principles in a more strict sense, do not aim to the direct realization of a goal; on the contrary, they perform the distinct function of prescribing and guiding some thought and argumentation processes, thus structuring the way rules and principles are applied. Hence, postulates are not located on the plane of rules and principles, but on a metaplane, which is the reason the author calls them second degree norms or application norms.

Notwithstanding the high level of abstraction and the density of the language and argumentation in a large part of the work, the presentation is enriched very elegantly with practical examples, taken from the Brazilian and German Law and found mostly in Constitutional and Tax Law, in accordance with the focus of the author's scientific work in substantive Law. Such fact also outlines the connection of his interest in legal theory to an ample legal-practical foundation – a combination that once again proves its fecundity in this work.

This is the reason it is my desire that this book be received in the German discussion about the Theory of Law with the interest and relevance it deserves.

Munich, August 2005

Prof. Dr. Dr. h.c. mult. Claus-Wilhelm Canaris
Professor of Civil Law and Science of Law Methodology
at the University of Munich, Germany.
Doctor Honoris Causa at the Universities of Lisbon,
Autonomous of Madrid, Athens and Graz.

FOREWORD TO THE BRAZILIAN EDITION (TEORIA DOS PRINCÍPIOS)

I called HUMBERTO as soon as I finished reading the book originals to tell him about my sincere admiration for the intellectual work it synthesized.

HUMBERTO has developed an extremely important contribution to what I would resort to French to call a *nettoyage* of jurisprudence. A conference I attended quite recently presented the distinction between interpretation methods, whether grammatical, teleological and so on. I suddenly realized that the lecturer was more than two hundred years old, truly an unburied corpse, to the sound of Ravel's *Bolero*...

HUMBERTO, as JOSÉ RÉGIO would say it, loves the distances and the mirages, the cliffs, the rapids, the deserts. When the soul is not small – quoting from RÉGIO to PESSOA – we shout the wonderful "I am not going this way; I am going only where my steps take me." This is it – I told HUMBERTO – "your book is a walk on your own steps." This book is personally his.

This is why this book is essential and truly breaks a trend that makes principles cliché, rocking the ground of the "self-geniuses." This is what they fear: when questioned, they react like one fighting for a life saver of some sort. Their problem is they have a single buoy, anchored to the bibliography of ages past – and poorly understood if more recent. They are common townsfolk, without a bibliography...

Let me tell a story. On the last day of the contest I took to become a Full Professor at Largo de São Francisco, as soon as the results were announced, another Professor, who had come from a different State and happened to be there, greeted me and said "This is great! Now you can sell your books!" To this day I do not know whether he meant it in jest or not. But I have the impression that some of them have traded their books long ago, and the buyers can now enjoy untouched old books never read before...

HUMBERTO's book fascinates me. It confirms my beliefs that interpretation is the interpretation/application of texts and facts and that balancing is a moment within the interpretation/application of the Law.

His guidelines for the analysis of principles – item 2.4.6 – make me see even more clearly that the Law is not interpreted in slices.

The proposition of a heuristic distinction between rule and principle – and postulates – and an "inclusive alternative" is extremely rich. And the tripartite model (rule, principle and applied normative postulate – item 3) illuminates the terrible darkness in which we know who gets lost. The exam of the postulate of proportionality is simply superb.

The text is multiple and varied, always in a positive way. The expounding of the principle of morality – item 2.4.7 – would have to be the first reading assignment for the half-baked "jurisprudents" who think morality replaces the ethic of statutory legality with another one, opposed to the statutes... What some have said in such matter is regrettable.

This is why I took the initiative to tell HUMBERTO that I would immensely love to write the foreword of this book – because then I would indirectly participate in the substantial contribution it brings up to our legal thinking. Being beside him makes me intellectually noble.

Prof. Dr. Eros Roberto Grau
Full Professor of Economic Law at the University of São Paulo. Justice of the Brazilian Supreme Court.

CONTENTS

CHAPTER 1

FIRST CONSIDERATIONS

The idea of writing this book sprang from the impact that previous articles on legal principles had on the legal environment.[1] One more reason joined: the permanent relevance of the distinction between principles and rules, which has been growing in jurisprudence and case law debates.

Public Law studies, mainly those of Constitutional Law, have significantly advanced concerning the interpretation and application of constitutional norms. Today, more than ever, it matters to construe the meaning and delimit the function of those norms which, setting forth goals to be achieved, work as the foundation for the application of the constitutional order — the legal principles. It is even possible to say that constitutional jurisprudence is currently excited about what has become known as a *State of Principles*. One must point out, however, that remarkable exceptions prove the rule that the excitement for novelty has brought on excesses and theoretical problems that have hindered legal order effectiveness. This is, mostly and paradoxically, about the effectiveness of elements called fundamental — the legal principles. Within that frame, some issues cause perplexity.

The first of them is the very distinction between principles and rules. On one hand, their distinctions due to structure and mode of application and collision believe as *necessary* some qualities that are merely *possible* to these normative species. Moreover, such distinctions emphasize the importance of principles, which eventually disparages the role of rules. On the other hand, these distinctions have given principles the status of norms that, being related to values that require subjective, personal analysis, can not be intersubjectively investigated in a controlled way. As a result, the indispensable discovery of which behaviors to adopt in order to realize principles is replaced with an investigation limited to the mere proclamation, at times desperate and inconsequent, of their importance. Principles are revered as the *bases* or *pillars* of the legal order, but no elements are accrued to this veneration that make their understanding and application better.

The second issue to provoke questioning is the lack of clear conceptual distinctions to manipulate the normative species. That happens not only because several different categories are used as synonyms, such as is the case of the indiscriminate references to *principles*, here and there mixed with *rules*, *axioms*, *postulates*, *ideas*, *measures*, *maxims*, and *criteria*, but also because many postulates, though distinct from one another as will be seen, are manipulated as if they required the same analysis from the interpreter, such as is the case of the uninformed allusion to *proportionality*, often mistaken for *fair proportion*, or *standard of reasonableness*, or the *prohibition of excess*, or the *equivalence relation*, or the *duty of weighing and balancing*, or the *duty of practical accordance*, or even *proportionality in a narrow sense* itself.

True, it is not the correct name of a principle what matters most. What is really decisive is to know the safest way to ensure its application and effectiveness. However, the application of the Law is dependent on those very institutional and speech processes without which it is not realized. The raw material interpreters use — the normative text or provision — is merely a legal possibility. The transformation of normative texts into legal norms depends on the interpreter's construing the meaning of their contents. These meanings, because of the duty of justifying the grounds for decisions, have to be understood by those manipulating them, which is even a condition to allow their addressees to understand them as well. This is exactly the reason why it is increasingly important to make distinctions among the categories judges use. Not only is the excessive use of categories opposed to a scientific requirement of accuracy, without which no science deserving its name can be built, but also it hinders the accuracy and predictability of Law, both of which are vital to keep the Rule of Law.

It is not hard to see, then, that this is not in order to praise a merely analytical requisite of distinction for the sake of separation. The names an interpreter gives to categories is of secondary matter. The need for distinction does not arise out of the existence of several names for numerous categories. It arises, instead, out of the need to give different phenomena different names.[2] This is not, therefore, a mere distinction of names, but a demand of conceptual accuracy: where there are many classes of exams from a practical view, it is advisable that they be classified differently as well.[3] Constitutional jurisprudence ought to seek accuracy as well because it affords better means to control governmental activity.[4]

This book, then, intends to help understand and apply principles and rules better. Its target is clear: to keep the distinction between principles and rules whereas structuring it on different foundations than those jurisprudence ordinarily employs. It will be shown, on one hand, that principles not only explicit values, but also set forth precise species of behaviors, though indirectly; on the other hand, the creation of conducts by rules is also to be weighed, even though the behavior set forth in advance may be overcome, depending on the accomplishment of a few requirements. That will surpass both the mere praise of values, which does not create behaviors, and the automatic application of rules. A model is proposed to explain the normative species, which includes structured weighing on the application process while encompassing substantive criteria of justice in its argument, through the analytical reconstruction of the concrete use of normative postulates, especially those of reasonableness and proportionality. All of that is done with a focus on the ability of intersubjective control of the argumentation, which often degenerates into capricious decisionism.

Distinguishing principles and rules has become fashionable. Public Law research, granted a few exceptions, deals with the distinction as if it were so obvious as to dispense with further comments. The separation among normative species seems to gain unanimity. And unanimity does not sow the seeds of critical knowledge of normative species, but rather the belief that they are like that, period.

It has become commonplace to state categorical distinctions between principles and rules. Norms are either principles or rules. Rules need not and can not be weighed; principles need and ought to be weighed. Rules set forth definitive commands, regardless of factual and normative possibilities; principles set forth preliminary commands, dependent on the factual and normative possibilities. When two rules collide, one of them is not valid, or else an exception should be made to one of them in order to overcome the conflict. When two principles collide, both overcome the conflict equally valid, and the judge must decide which one prevails.

The analysis of such statements, however, presents some doubts. Is it so that all normative species behave as principles or rules? Is it so that rules can not be weighed? Is it so that rules always set forth definitive commands? Is it so that the conflicts of rules are only solved if one of the rules is invalid or if an exception is made to one of them? This book not only answers these and many other questions that arise out of the analysis of the distinction between principles and rules, but it also presents a new paradigm to distinguish and apply normative species.

Truly enough, while scholars in general understand there is interpretation of rules and weighing of principles, this work criticizes that separation and attempts to show it is possible to weigh in rules as well. While scholars sustain that the consequence of a rule ought to be implemented when its condition is met, this study differentiates the incidence of rules from their applicability in order to show that a number of factors are to be weighed in to enable the application of a rule which go beyond merely verifying that facts established previously have happened. While scholars sustain that a given provision is exclusively either a rule or a principle, this research defends inclusive alternatives within species at times generated from a single provision. While scholars refer to proportionality and reasonableness sometimes as principles and sometimes as rules, this work criticizes these conceptions and, deepening a previous study, proposes a new category called normative applicative postulates. While scholars equal reasonableness and proportionality, this study criticizes such model and explains why it can not be upheld. While scholars understand reasonableness as a field with no structure or normative basis, this investigation retraces decisions to give them a doctrinal standing. While scholars equal the prohibition of excess and proportionality in a narrow sense, this study distinguishes them and explains why they are distinct species of argumentative control. This is all done in as straightforward a way as possible, including examples in the course of the arguments.

By doing so, conditions are created that incorporate justice into the legal debate, without risking the consistency of the arguments.

In order to do that, the first object of investigation is the phenomenon of interpretation in Law. The aim here is to understand that the classification of certain normative species as either *principles* or *rules* depends in the first place on axiological connections that are not ready prior to the interpretation process that unveils them. Then, a definition of *principles* is proposed, aiming to understand what their unique characteristics are when compared to other norms of the legal order. Thirdly, the conditions for the application of principles and rules are examined, which are the normative applicative postulates.

NOTES

1. ÁVILA, Humberto Bergmann. A distinção entre princípios e regras e a redefinição do dever de proporcionalidade. *Revista de Direito Administrativo* (215):151–179, Rio de Janeiro: Renovar, jan./mar. 1999. Idem. Repensando o princípio da supremacia do interesse público sobre o particular. *Revista Trimestral de Direito Público* (24):159–180, São Paulo: Malheiros, 1999.
2. ÁVILA, Humberto Bergmann. A distinção entre princípios e regras e a redefinição do dever de proporcionalidade. *RDA* (215):151–152, Rio de Janeiro: Renovar, jan./mar. 1999.
3. HUSTER, Stefan. *Rechte und Ziele: Zur Dogmatik des allgemeinen Gleichheitssatzes*. Berlin: Duncker und Humblot, 1993. p. 134, 144 and 145.
4. VOGEL, Klaus/WALDHOFF, Christian. *Grundlagen des Finanzverfassungsrechts: Sonderausgabe des Bonner Kommentars zum Grundgesetz (Vorbemerkungen zu Art. 104a bis 115 GG)*. Heidelberg: Müller, 1999. margin number 342, p. 232.

CHAPTER 2

NORMS

Principles And Rules

2.1. FIRST DISTINCTIONS

2.1.1. Text and Norm

Norms are neither text nor a set of texts, but the meanings construed from the systematic interpretation of normative texts. Therefore, one can say that provisions are the object of interpretation and norms are its result.[1] What matters is that there is no correspondence between norm and provision in the sense that where there is a provision there is a norm, or that where there is a norm there is a provision to support it.

In some cases, there is a norm, but no provision. Which provision set forth the principles of legal stability and certainty of decisions? None. So, there are norms even without specific provisions to support them physically.

In other cases, there is a provision, but there is no norm. Which norm can be construed from the constitutionally stated *protection of God*? None. So, there are provisions from which no norm is construed.

In other cases, there is only one provision from which more than one norm is construed. A good example is the prescriptive statement that requires a statute to create or increase taxes, which derives the principle of statutory legality, the principle of legal certainty, the prohibition of independent regulations and the prohibition of normative delegation. Another example that illustrates that is the declaration of partial unconstitutionality without text editing: when STF, the Brazilian Supreme Court, examines the constitutionality of norms, it investigates the various meanings that comprise the definition of a given provision, and declares, without altering the text, the unconstitutionality of those that are incompatible with the Federal Constitution. The provision is kept, but the norms construed upon it which are incompatible with the Federal Constitution are declared void. So, there are provisions from which more than one norm can be construed.

In other cases, there are two or more provisions, but only one norm is construed from them. The examination of the provisions that warrant statutory legality, irretroactivity, and previous enactment derives the principle of legal stability. Hence, there can be more than one provision and a single norm construed.

What does it mean? It means that there is no one-to-one correspondence between provision and norm, i.e., where there is one, there need not be the other.

2.1.2. Description, Construction and Reconstruction

Reflections such as these that point to a separation between the text and its meaning also lead to the conclusion that the function of Jurisprudence can not be considered a mere description of meaning, either from the perspective of communicating information or knowledge concerning a text or from that of the author's intention.

On one hand, understanding its meaning as the conceptual content of a text presupposes the existence of an intrinsic meaning that is independent from use or interpretation. That, however, does not occur, because meaning is not something incorporated into the content of words; rather, it is dependent precisely on their use and interpretation, as shown by the changes in the meaning of terms over time and space and the scholar controversies regarding the most appropriate meaning a statute should be given. On the other hand, the concept that nears meaning to the intention of the legislator presupposes the existence of a distinct author and a univocal intention to lay the foundations of the text. That is not so, however, because the legislation process is defined exactly as a complex process that is not subjected to an individual author or to a specific will. Therefore, interpretation is not an act of describing a meaning previously assigned; rather, it is a decision that *creates* the signification and meanings of a text.[2] The core matter of all that is that interpreters do not assign legal terms "the" correct meaning thereof. Interpreters simply build examples of language use or versions of signification — meanings —, since language is never given beforehand; rather, it becomes concrete in use, or better, as used.[3]

These considerations lead to an understanding that the activity of interpreters — whether judges or scholars — is not merely to describe the previously existing meaning of provisions. Their activity is comprised of creating such meanings.[4] Because of that, it is not plausible either to accept the idea that the application of the law involves the coupling of concepts that were ready prior to the application process.[5]

However, verifying that interpreters construe meanings within the interpretation process should not lead to the conclusion that there is no meaning at all before such interpretation process is over. Stating that meaning is dependent on use is not the same as maintaining that it only arises from specific, individual use. This is so because there are minimum traces of meaning incorporated to the ordinary or technical uses of language. WITTGENSTEIN refers to *language games*: some meanings are preexistent to the particular process of interpretation, as they result from content stereotypes already present in general linguistic communication.[6] HEIDEGGER mentions the *hermeneutical "as"*: there are *a priori* or previous comprehension structures that enable a minimum understanding of each sentence from a certain point of view that was previously incorporated into the common use of language.[7] REALE uses the *intersubjective a priori condition*: there are preexistent structural conditions in the cognition process that cause individuals to interpret something previously presented to them.[8] One can thus state that the common use of language creates some conditions of use of the language itself. As AARNIO reminds us, terms such as *life*, *death*, *mother*, *before*, *after* have *intersubjectivized meanings* that do not have to be explained at every instance. They operate as given conditions of communication.[9]

Consequently, one can thus say that interpreters not only build, but also *rebuild* meaning, given the existence of significations incorporated to language use and built within the community of the speech. Expressions such as *provisional* or *extensive*, despite having inexact significations, have meaning cores that allow one to point out, at least, those situations where they do not apply: a remedy is not provisional if its effects protract along time; defense is not extensive unless it has all means required to realize it. And so forth. This is why it is said that to interpret is *to build from something*, and so it means *to rebuild*: firstly, because its starting point is the normative texts, which place limits to the construction of meanings; secondly, it manipulates language, incorporating *meaning cores* that are created by use, so to speak, and preexistent to the individual interpretation process.

The commonplace conclusion is that judges and jurisprudence build meanings, but face limits that, if disregarded, disjoint constitutional provisions and the actual Constitutional Law. When one understands *provisional* as *permanent*, *thirty days* as *more than thirty days*, *all resources* as *some resources*, *extensive defense* as *restricted defense*, *effective display of economic capacity* as *probable display of economic capacity*, one does not realize the constitutional text. One pretends to realize it by disdaining its minimum meanings. This verification explains why scholars have so plentifully criticized some decisions made by the Brazilian Supreme Court.

Besides leading to the conclusions above, this demonstration also requires the replacement of some traditional beliefs with more solid knowledge: one needs to replace the conviction that provisions equal norms by verifying that a provision is the starting point of interpretation; one needs to surpass the belief that an interpreter's role is merely to describe signification and understand that interpreters rebuild meanings, whether they be scientists building syntactic and semantic connections or judges, who add circumstances of the cases they adjudicate to those connections; one needs to dismiss the opinion that the Judiciary only plays the role of negative legislator and understand that it realizes the legal order in real, concrete cases.[10]

In sum, it is exactly because interpreters build norms from provisions that one cannot conclude that this or that provision *contains* a rule or principle within. This normative qualification depends on axiological connections that are not incorporated into the text, neither belong to it; rather, they are built by interpreters themselves. That does not mean, as already stated, that interpreters are free to make the connections between norms and the ends they aim at. The legal order sets forth the realization of purposes, the preservation of values, and the upholding of and the search for some legal assets essential to the realization of such purposes and preservation of such values. Interpreters cannot disregard these starting points. This is exactly why the act of interpretation is best translated as an act of *reconstruction*: interpreters must interpret constitutional provisions in a way to explicit their versions of signification according to the purposes and values somehow shown in the constitutional language.

What is essential this far is to know that the classification of some norms as *principles* or *rules* depends on the creative collaboration of interpreters. What is yet to know is how to define principles and what proposition is hereby defended.

2.2. AN OVERVIEW OF THE EVOLUTION OF THE DISTINCTION BETWEEN PRINCIPLES AND RULES

Several writers have proposed definitions for the normative species, some of which have greatly impacted on scholars. The scope of this study is not to investigate all concepts concerning the distinction between principles and rules, or even to examine the whole work of some of the most important advocates.[11] The goal of this work is, firstly, to describe the foundations of the most important works on the topic, and, secondly, to analyze the distinction criteria chosen both objectively and critically.

For ESSER, principles are those norms that set forth the grounds for a given commandment to be found.[12] More than a distinction based on the degree of abstraction of the normative provision, the difference between principles and rules would be a qualitative distinction.[13] The criterion that distinguishes principles and rules would then be the role of normative foundation for making decisions.

In line with that, LARENZ defines principles as norms of great relevance to the legal order, since they set forth normative grounds for the interpretation and application of Law which directly or indirectly derive behavior norms.[14] For him, principles would be directive thoughts of a possible or existing legal regulation, but still not applicable rules because they lack the formal aspect of legal propositions, i.e., the connection between an *operative fact* and a *legal consequence*. This is why principles would only show the way for the rule to be found, as if setting a first guiding step to the other steps that lead to the rule.[15] The criterion that distinguishes principles and rules would also be the role of normative foundation for making decisions, a quality derived from the conditional pattern of drafting normative prescriptions.

According to CANARIS, two attributes tell principles apart from rules. First, the axiological content: principles, as opposed to rules, have explicit axiological content and therefore lack rules in order to be realized. Secondly, there is the way they interact with other norms: principles, as opposed to rules, receive their meaning content only by means of a dialectic process of complementation and limitation.[16] Thus, new elements are added to the distinctive criteria mentioned before, because the foundation role that principles play is qualified as axiological and their interactive mode is considered distinctive.

It was the Anglo-Saxon tradition that gave a vigorous contribution to the definition of principles.[17] The aim of DWORKIN's study was to thrust a general attack on positivism, mostly concerning the open kind of argumentation allowed by the application of what he defined as principles.[18] For him, rules are applied as all or nothing, in the sense that if the operative fact of a rule occurs, then the rule is valid and its normative consequence ought to be accepted or else it is not considered valid. In case rules collide, one of them ought to be considered invalid. Principles, otherwise, do not define the decision at all; rather, they only contain foundations that ought to be combined with other foundations derived from other principles.[19] Therefore comes the statement that principles, as opposed to rules, have a certain dimension of weight, demonstrated when principles collide, in which case the principle with greater relative weight superposes the other, without the latter losing its validity.[20] This wise, the distinction DWORKIN elaborated is not one of degree, but one concerning logical structure, based on classifying rather than comparing criteria, as ALEXY states.[21] The distinction he proposes differs from the previous ones because it is more intensely based on the mode of application and normative relation, thus further contrasting these two normative species.

ALEXY, setting off from DWORKIN's considerations, defined the concept of principles even more precisely. For him, legal principles consist only of a species of legal norms through which optimization commands are set forth that are applicable at several degrees, according to normative and factual possibilities.[22] Taking the precedents of the German Constitutional Court as his basis, ALEXY shows the tense relation occurring when principles collide: in such case, the solution is not solved with the immediate decision that a principle takes precedence over another, but it is set forth as a result of weighing the colliding principles, where one takes precedence because of specific actual circumstances.[23] Principles, therefore, have a dimension of weight only, and do not directly determine the normative consequences directly, as opposed to rules.[24] Principles are only realized through their application in real, concrete cases by means of collision rules. Therefore, the application of a principle must always be seen with some reservation, defined as "*if no other principle has a greater weight in the concrete case.*"[25] That is to say: the weighing of conflicting principles is solved by the creation of prevalence rules, which causes principles, then, to be applied as *all or nothing* ("*Alles-oder-Nichts*") as well.[26] This kind of tension and the way it is resolved is what tells principles apart from rules: whereas in the conflict between rules, one must verify whether the rule is within or without a given legal order (*within or without problem*), the conflict between principles is placed within that same order (*theorem of collision*).[27]

That brings up the definition of principles as *optimization commands* applicable at several degrees according to normative and factual possibilities: normative because the application of principles depends on principles and rules opposed to them, and factual because the content of principles as norms of conduct can only be determined when faced with facts. Something different happens with rules. "*On the other hand, rules are norms that may be realized or not. When a rule is valid, it is then determined that whatever it requires be done, nothing more and nothing less.*"[28] Legal rules, as stated, are norms whose premises are directly met or not, and when colliding the contradiction will be solved by introducing an exception to the rule, therefore excluding the conflict, or by declaring one of the rules invalid.[29]

The distinction between principles and rules, according to ALEXY, can not be based on the *all or nothing* application standard DWORKIN proposes; rather, it must be restricted to two factors: *difference concerning collision*, as colliding principles have their normative realization limited reciprocally only, as opposed to rules, whose collision is solved by declaring one of them invalid or by creating an exception that eliminates the contradiction; and *difference concerning the obligation set forth*, since rules set forth absolute obligations, not overcome by opposed norms, whereas principles set forth *prima facie* obligations that can be overcome or preempted due to other colliding principles.[30]

This jurisprudential evolution, besides showing weak (ESSER, LARENZ, CANARIS) and strong (DWORKIN, ALEXY) distinctions between principles and rules, shows that the criteria usually employed for such distinction are the following.

First of all, there is the *hypothetical-conditional aspect*, based on the fact that rules present a condition and a consequence that preset the decision, being applied in an *if, then* fashion, whereas principles only point to the foundation a judge can use to find the rule for the real case eventually. DWORKIN states: "*If the facts a rule stipulates are given, then either the rule is valid, in which case the answer it supplies ought to be accepted, or it is not, in which case it contributes nothing to the decision.*"[31] ALEXY follows a similar path when he defines rules as norms whose premises are, or are not, directly fulfilled.[32]

Secondly, there is the *final mode of application*, supported by the fact that rules are applied in an absolute *all or nothing* mode, whereas principles are applied in a gradual *more or less* mode.

Thirdly, the *normative relation*, based on the idea that the contradiction between rules embodies a true conflict, which can be solved by declaring one of the rules invalid or by creating an exception, whereas the relation between principles consists of a juxtaposition, which can be solved with weighing that assigns each of them a dimension of weight.

Fourthly, there is the *axiological foundation*, which considers principles, as opposed to rules, as axiological foundations for the decision to be made.

All these distinction criteria are important, since they point to qualities worthy of examination by Jurisprudence. That does not prevent us, however, from investigating ways to improve them, not in a sense to downplay their importance, or even less to deny the merits of the works that examined them, but in a sense that reaffirms their worth with the most appropriate means to show esteem and scientific respect: criticism.

2.3. PRINCIPLES AND RULES DISTINCTION CRITERIA

2.3.1. Hypothetical-conditional Aspect

2.3.1.1. Content According to some scholars, principles could be distinguished from rules by their *hypothetical conditional character*, because they understand that rules present a hypothesis (condition) and a consequence that predetermine the decision, being applied in an *if-then* fashion, whereas principles only point the grounds which a judge can use in order to find the rule that eventually applies to the concrete case.

ESSER defined principles as norms that set forth bases for a given commandment to be found, whereas in his opinion rules determine the decision itself.[33] LARENZ defined principles as norms of great relevance for the legal order inasmuch as they set forth normative foundations for the interpretation and application of the Law, therefrom evolving, whether directly or indirectly, behavior norms.[34]

2.3.1.2. Critical analysis The differentiation criterion regarding the *hypothetical-conditional character* is relevant in that it lets one see that rules have one clear, up-front descriptive element, whereas principles only set forth a directive. This criterion, though, is not void of criticism.

First of all, this criterion is imprecise. Truly, even though it is right to say that principles point to a first guiding step for new steps in order to obtain the rule ultimately, this distinction does not provide a basis to show what it means to give a *first step* to find the rule. Put this way, this distinction criterion still contributes for the judge to understand the rule as providing, from the start, the *last step* to discovering the normative content. That, however, is not true in that the normative content of any norm, whether a rule or a principle, depends on the normative and factual possibilities to be verified in the very process of applying it. Therefore, the *last step* is not given neither by the provision nor by the preliminary meaning of the norm, but by the interpretative decision, as will be further explored later on.

Secondly, the existence of operative facts is a matter of linguistic formulation and therefore it cannot be a distinctive element of a normative species. Indeed, some norms that one can classify as principles, according to the criterion, can be *rewritten* in a conditional way, as the following examples show: "*if* the governmental power is practiced, *then* democratic participation ought to be assured" (principle of democracy); "*if* the requirement of observing the operative facts of norms that set forth obligations is not met, *then* the acts of the administration will be considered void" (principle of legal certainty).[35]

These examples show that the existence of a hypothesis is more dependent on the way one writes them than on a characteristic empirically assigned to only one category of norms. Besides that, the "*hypothetical-conditional character*" criterion presupposes that the kind of norm and its normative attributes are a necessary consequence of the wording of the provision under interpretation, as if the way a provision is manifest (object of the interpretation) completely predetermined they way the norm (result of the interpretation) will regulate the human conduct or the way it will be applied. One can notice a clear confusion between provision and norm and an obvious transposition of attributes from the statements the legislator expressed to the statements the judge expresses.

Secondly, even if the legislature has created a given provision as a condition, that does not mean the interpreter can not understand it as a principle. The relation between constitutional norms and the purposes and values used to make them come true is not complete before interpretation, neither is it incorporated to the constitutional text itself before interpretation. This relation ought to be coherently built by the interpreter within the textual and contextual limits. Therefore, it is not correct to say that a constitutional provision *contains* or *is* a principle or a rule, or that a given provision ought to be considered a principle or a rule because it has been formulated in a given way. Since interpreters have the task of measuring and specifying the intensity of the relation between the provision they interpret and the purposes and values overlying it potentially and axiologically, they can legally interpret a provision formulated in theory to be a rule or a principle. It all depends on the connections of value that interpreters stress or not with their argumentation, and on the goals they believe should be met. To do so, one can simply check some examples of provisions formulated in theory that can seem to be either rules of principles.

The constitutional provision stating that *if* a tax is created or raised *then* such creation or raise ought to be enacted by statute is applied as a *rule* if the judge sees its immediate behavioral aspect and understands it as a mere legal, formal requirement to validate the creation or raise of taxes; likewise, it can be understood as a *principle* if the judge, acting freely from the behavior followed in the legislative process, focuses on the teleological aspect and realizes it as a means to achieve *freedom* that allows tax planning and forbids taxation by analogy, and as a means to achieve *stability*, in order to assure foreseeability by legally setting forth the elements of tax obligations and to forbid the enactment of rules that go over the limits initially set.

The constitutional provision, according to which *if* taxes are created or raised *then* taxable events occurred after the enactment of the statute that has created or raised such taxes are the only events to be considered, is applied as a *rule* if the judge understands it as a mere requirement of publishing the statute before the taxable events occur, and it can be understood as a *principle* if the judge brings it to life with the purpose of accomplishing the value *stability* to forbid a tax raise in the middle of a fiscal year in which a time-protracted event has already begun, or with the goal of accomplishing the value *trust* in order to forbid individual raises of tax rates when the Administration has already entered a decree promising to lower them.

The constitutional provision, according to which *if* taxes are created or raised *then* they can not be collected until the beginning of a new fiscal year, is applied as a *rule* if the judge understands it as a mere requirement of publishing the statute before a new fiscal year begins, and it can be understood as a *principle* if the judge brings it to life with the purpose of accomplishing the value *foreseeability* in order to forbid tax raises when taxpayers do not have the least actual condition to know about the content of the norms they will be subject to, or to postpone the resumption of collection of a tax whose exemption has been revoked in the course of the fiscal year.

The examples referred to above prove that what matters in classifying a norm as a principle is not the fact that it has been construed from a provision set forth as a normative hypothesis that is supposedly defined. On one hand, any norm can be reformulated so as to present an operative fact followed by a consequence.[36] On the other hand, any norm, even those presenting a condition followed by a consequence, may refer purposes. Thus, the classification as either principle or rule depends on its argumentative use, and not on the hypothetical structure.[37]

Besides that, it is not correct to state that principles are opposed to rules in that the former have neither normative consequences nor operative facts. Principles also have normative consequences. On one hand, the reason (end, purpose, task) to which the principle refers ought to be considered relevant in a real case.[38] On the other hand, the behavior needed to accomplish or preserve a certain ideal state of affairs (*Idealzustand*) ought to be adopted.[39] The duties to assign relevance to the purpose being sought and to adopt the behaviors necessary to accomplish the goals are extremely important normative consequences. Moreover, even though principles do not have a clear aspect of behavior description, it can not be denied that their interpretation, even at an abstract level, may show the kinds of behaviors to be adopted, especially if the most important cases are rebuilt.

The key point, then, is not the lack of prescriptions of behaviors and consequences in the case of principles, but the kind of prescriptions of behaviors and consequences, which is something else.

2.3.2. Final Mode of Application

2.3.2.1. Content According to some scholars, principles could be distinguished from rules by their *final mode of application*, because they understand that rules are applied in an absolute *all or nothing* mode, whereas principles are applied in a gradual *more or less* mode.

DWORKIN says that rules are applied in *all-or-nothing* mode, in the sense that if the condition for the incidence of a rule is met, then the rule is valid and its normative consequence ought to be accepted or else it is not considered valid. Principles, otherwise, do not define the decision at all; rather, they only contain foundations that ought to be combined with other foundations derived from other principles.[40] According to him, if the facts set by a rule do occur, then either the rule is valid, in which case the answer it offers ought to be accepted, or else an exception to this rule ought to be found.[41]

ALEXY defines rules as norms whose premises are, or are not, directly fulfilled.[42] According to him, rules set forth absolute obligations, as long as not overcome by opposed norms, whereas principles set forth *prima facie* obligations in that they can be overcome or preempted due to other colliding principles.[43]

2.3.2.2. Critical analysis The *final mode of application* criterion, despite having drawn attention to important aspects of legal norms, can be partially rewritten. Let us see.

Firstly, one needs to show that the mode of application is not determined by the text under interpretation, but derives from the axiological connections that are construed (or at least coherently stressed) by the interpreter, who may invert the mode of application initially considered elementary. Indeed, the absolute aspect of the rule is very often completely modified after all circumstances of the case are considered. It is enough to examine a few cases of norms that initially point to an absolute mode of application, but upon consideration of all circumstances end up requiring a complex process of reasoning and counter-reasoning.

On one hand, there are norms whose preliminary normative content sets forth objective limits that, if not complied with, apparently impose the absolute implementation of the consequence. This obligation, called *absolute*, does not hinder other contrary reasons that may overlap in some cases, however. Let us see some examples.

The norm construed from article 224 of the Brazilian Penal Code, upon setting forth provisions for the crime of rape, enacts an unconditional assumption of violence in case the victim is below 14 years of age. *If* one has sexual relations with a minor of 14 years of age or less, *then* it ought to be assumed the actor acted violently. The norm does not set forth any exception. Such norm, under the classifying standard examined here, would be a rule and therefore enact an absolute obligation: if the victim is 14 or less, and the rule is valid, rape and assumed violence ought to be acknowledged. However, the Brazilian Supreme Court (STF), when trying a case in which the victim was 12 years old, placed such relevance to *particular circumstances not regulated by the norm*, such as victim's consent and her physical and mental older appearance, that it decided the crime was not configured although the express normative requirements were found.[44] This means that the application showed that that obligation, considered absolute, was overcome by contrary reasons *not regulated by the norm or any other reason.*

The norm built from article 37, item II of the Federal Constitution sets forth that the installation in public office or employment is dependent on previous approbation in a public contest of exams or exams and honors. *If* a public servant is admitted into the Administration, *then* the corresponding installation must follow a public contest; otherwise, such installation shall be declared void. In addition, the person who effected admission will have committed a statutory act of dishonest administration, which faces several consequences, including the filing of a fitting criminal action. However, the Brazilian Supreme Court did not proceed with prosecution in the case of a city Mayor who was charged with this felony because when she ran a City Administration she hired a citizen, without a public contest, to provide cleaning services as a street sweeper for a period of nine months. Upon adjudication of her *habeas corpus*, no damage to the Municipality was found as a result of her single act. Also, it was considered offensive to the natural order of things, and therefore to the postulate of reasonableness, to require a public contest to hire a single person to perform an activity of minor rank.[45] In this case, a condition – according to which a public contest is required before hiring a public servant – was met, but the consequence of its non-compliance was not implemented (voiding the installation and, due to another norm, occurrence of an act of dishonest administration) because not using the behavior it set forth would not damage the advancement of the purpose that justifies its existence (protection of public assets). In other words: according to the decision, public assets will still be protected even if a single street sweeper is hired for a certain time.

Federal tax legislation had a rule according to which a company accepted into the simplified federal tax payment program was forbidden to import foreign products. *If* it imported, *then* the company would be excluded from the simplified payment program. A small sofa manufacturer, classified as small for the purposes of paying federal taxes in a single operation, was excluded from this scheme because it violated the legal condition of not importing foreign products. Indeed, this company imported once. However, it imported four legs for a single sofa – only once. Upon appeal, that exclusion was reversed because a *reasonable interpretation* means interpretation should be "in accordance with that which common sense would understand as acceptable before the Law."[46] In this case, the condition was met according to which imports are forbidden if a company is to remain under special tax rules, but the consequence of its non-compliance was not implemented (exclusion from that special tax program) because not using the behavior set forth would not damage the advancement of the purpose that justified its existence (assisting small companies to increase national production). In other words: according to the decision, the national production will still be assisted even if a few legs for a sofa are imported.

The cases mentioned above, to which others could be added, show that the consequence set forth *prima facie* by the norm can be deferred due to substantive reasons a judge chooses, upon proper justification, to consider superior to those that justify the rule itself. One can either examine the rule's purpose in order to understand and therefore restrict or expand the meaning content of the normative hypothesis, or refer to other reasons, based on other norms, that justify overruling that rule. These considerations are enough to show that it is not appropriate to state rules as "having" an absolute "all or nothing" mode of application. Also, the rules that seem to point to an unconditional mode of application can be overruled by reasons unimaginable to the legislator in ordinary cases. Taking real, individual circumstances into consideration is not about the structure of norms, but about their application; principles as well as rules can involve the consideration of specific aspects which were not considered in abstract.[47]

On the other hand, there are rules that contain expressions whose scope of application is not (completely and previously) delimited, the judge being in charge of deciding whether the norm is met in each real case. In these situations, the absolute character of the rule is lost in favor of a *more or less* mode of application. Electronic books are a good example that only a complex process of weighing arguments for and against their inclusion in the sphere of constitutional tax exemption will allow one to decide in favor of it.[48]

All of these reflections show that it only makes sense to say that rules are applied as *all or nothing* when all questions related to the validity, meaning and final coupling of facts and rules are settled.[49] Even in the case of rules, these questions are not easily answered. That is so because vagueness is not a distinctive character of principles, but a common element of any provisional statement, whether it is a principle or a rule.[50]

Likewise, it is important to notice that the specific characteristic of rules (the implementation of a preset consequence) can only arise after they are interpreted. Only then can one understand if and which consequences will supposedly be implemented in case they are applied to a real case. That means the distinction between principles and rules can not be based on the accepted *all or nothing* method of applying rules because rules that are to have their consequences implemented also need a previous process of interpretation — which can be as long and complex as the process of principles —, and such process will show which consequences will be implemented. And even so, only the application in a real case will confirm the hypothesis previously seen as automatic. This way, upon interpretation that weighs in specific circumstances (the act of application), rules and principles tend to blend instead of contrasting.[51] The only verifiable difference is again the degree of abstraction prior to the interpretation (which also depends on previous interpretation to verify): in the case of principles, the degree of abstraction is greater in relation to the behavior norm to be determined, since principles are not abstractly bound to a specific situation (e.g., principle of democracy, the rule of Law); in the case of rules, consequences are immediately identifiable, although they ought to be confirmed by their application. This distinction criterion between principles and rules becomes less relevant, though, when it is verified that, on one hand, the application of rules also depends on the parallel interpretation of the principles referring to them (e.g. the rules of the legislation process are related to the principle of democracy) and that, on the other hand, principles usually require the complementation of rules in order to be applied.

What matters is that principles as well as rules are open to the reflection on real and individual aspects. In the case of principles, such reflection on real and individual aspects does not have institutional impediments, since principles set forth a *state of affairs* that is aimed at, but do not directly describe which behaviors lead to it. It is interesting that the goal, regardless of authority, works as the substantive reason to adopt the behaviors necessary to its promotion. A given behavior is adopted because its effects contribute to the promotion of a goal. Principles could be classified as norms that generate substantive reasons or goal reasons to argue for.[52] For example, the interpretation of the principle of morality will show that seriousness, justification and loyalty make up the general state of affairs, and that serious, clarifying and loyal behaviors are necessary. The principle, however, will not show what exactly these behaviors are.

As for rules, attention to concrete, individual aspects can only be given upon grounds that enable escaping the *trap* of understanding that rules ought to be obeyed.[53] It is the rule itself that operates as the reason to adopt the behavior. A behavior is adopted because, regardless of its effects, it is correct. The authority deriving from the enactment of the rule operates as the reason to act. Rules could be classified as norms that create rightness reasons or authority reasons for the argumentation. Going further on a previous example, sexual violence would no longer be assumed only if there were exceptional reasons with a strong sense of justification, such as the victim's open consent or her physical or mental older appearance. In other words, in the case of the application of rules, the judge can also consider specific elements of each situation, although using them depends on an argumentation burden capable of overcoming the reason to obey the rule. Weighing is, therefore, necessary. That means that the distinctive trace is not the kind of obligation the conditional structure of the norm creates, absolute or relative, which will classify it into one normative species or another. It is the way the judges justify the application of the preliminary signification of a provision, whether up-front finalistic or behavioral, that enables the classification as this or that normative species.

One should point out, however, that neither is it coherent to state that, as DWORKIN and ALEXY do, each in his own way, if the condition set forth in a rule does occur in fact, the normative consequence ought to be directly implemented.[54] On one hand, there are cases in which rules can be applied without their conditions being met. Such is the case of the application of rules by analogy: in these cases, the conditions of rule applicability are not implemented, but they are still applied because the non-regulated cases are similar to the cases set forth by the normative conditions, thus justifying application of the rule. And there are cases in which rules are not applied although their conditions have been met. Such is the case of canceling the justifying purpose by a reason the judge considers superior in a given real case.[55] That means that sometimes the conditions of rule applicability are not met and the rule is still applied, and sometimes these conditions are met and the rule is not applied anyway. Strictly speaking, therefore, it is not plausible to defend that rules are norms whose application is sure when their operative facts occur.

It is also common to say that rules are applied or not in whole, whereas principles can be more or less applied. It is an interesting proposition, but it can be improved. Truly, when one affirms that rules are applied wholly, the described behavior is seen as one that can occur or not; when one argues that principles are applied *more or less*, one focuses his analysis on the state of affairs that can be reached because the due behavior is not described. That means, however, that it is not so that principles are applied gradually, *more or less*, but it is the state of affairs that can be more or less approximated, depending on the conduct chosen as medium. Even under this hypothesis, a principle is either applied or not: either the behavior required to realize or preserve the state of affairs is adopted or it is not adopted. Therefore, arguing that principles are applied gradually is to mistake the norm for its external aspects, required to apply it.

The main point is not, then, the supposedly absolute character of the obligations created by rules, but the way one can validly overcome the reasons that implement their consequences; neither is it a lack of attention to concrete, individual aspects in rules, but the way such attention ought to be validly justified, which is something else.

2.3.3. Normative Conflict

2.3.3.1. Content According to some scholars, principles could be distinguished from rules by the way they work in the case of *normative conflicts*, because they understand the contradiction of rules carries in itself a true conflict that is to be resolved by declaring one of the rules to be invalid or by creating an exception, whereas the correlation of principles is a juxtaposition, which can be solved with balancing that assigns each of them a dimension of weight.

CANARIS, besides making the axiological content of principles clear, distinguishes principles and rules based on their interaction with other norms: principles, as opposed to rules, would receive their content of meaning only by means of a dialectical process of complementation and limitation.[56]

DWORKIN argues that principles, as opposed to rules, have a dimension of weight that is manifested in case of collision, in which case the principle with relatively more weight superimposes on the other without the latter losing validity.[57]

ALEXY argues that legal principles consist only of one species of legal norms through which optimization commands are set which are applicable in several degrees, according to norm and fact possibilities.[58] In case principles collide, the solution is not to determine immediately that one principle prevails over the other, but it is found by weighing the colliding principles and then one of them, in some actual circumstances, will prevail.[59] This kind of tension and the way it is resolved is what distinguishes principles from rules: while in the conflict of rules one needs to find out whether the rule is within or without some legal order, in the conflict of principles this very order has such conflict within itself.[60]

2.3.3.2. Critical analysis Analyzing the *normative conflict* is also a decisive step in perfecting the study of normative species. Despite that, it needs improvement. This is so because it is not appropriate to say that weighing is an exclusive method of principle application, nor that principles have a dimension of weight.

Truly, weighing is not an exclusive method of principle application. Weighing and balancing (*Abwägung*), which is to counterweigh the pros and cons that climax with the decision of interpretation, can also be present in hypothetically written provisions, whose application is previously considered automatic (in the case of rules, according to the criterion now under investigation), as the analysis of some examples demonstrates.

First of all, weighing is an activity that ensues when rules coexist abstractly, but may actually conflict with each other. It is common to say that there are two options when two rules conflict with each other: either one of the rules is declared void, or an exception is created in order to go around their incompatibility. Because of that, it is argued that rules conflict at an abstract level and that the solution to that conflict is part of the norm validity problem. Now, when two principles conflict with each other, one must assign one of them a greater dimension of weight. Therefore, it is pleaded that principles conflict at a concrete level and that the solution to that conflict is part of the application problem.

However tempting and widely advertised, this understanding deserves rethinking. This is because, in some cases, rules are in mutual conflict, but remain valid, and the solution to the conflict depends on assigning one of them a greater dimension of weight. Two examples may clarify that.

First example: a rule in the Medical Ethics Code states that doctors must tell their patients all the truth concerning their diseases, and another states that doctors must use all available means to cure their patients. But what is there to do when telling the truth about a disease will decrease their chances of cure due to the consequent emotional impact? Should the doctor tell the truth or hide it? Cases such as this not only show that conflicts of rules are not necessarily set at abstract levels, and may arise actually as those of principles. Such cases also show that the decision involves counterweighing pros and cons.[61]

Second example: a rule forbids the awarding of preliminary specific performance by the Public Treasury if such award exhausts the matter under litigation (first article of Act 9.494/97). That rule *prohibits* judges from preliminarily ordering the health system to supply medicine to those who need it to survive. Another rule, however, sets forth that the government must supply exceptional medicine, at no cost, to the people who can not bear the respective cost (first article of State Act 9.908/93). This rule *tells* the judge to order the health system, even preliminarily and before exhaustion of discovery, to supply medicine to those who need it to survive.[62] Even though these rules create contradictory behaviors where one sets forth a behavior that the other forbids, they go beyond the abstract conflict and *keep their validity*. It is not absolutely necessary to void one of the rules or make an exception to one of them. It is not required to place a rule within and a rule without the legal order. What happens is an actual conflict of rules such that the judge must assign greater weight to one of the two because of the goal each one intends to preserve: either the goal of preserving the lives of citizens prevails or the goal of ensuring an immovable public budget superimposes. Regardless of the solution, which is not under analysis here, this is a concrete conflict of rules whose solution is not found at a level of validity but at a level of application, and thus dependent on weighing the goals in jeopardy.

Thus, one needs to improve the understanding that the conflict of rules is necessarily abstract and that when two rules conflict, then one ought to be void or an exception ought to be created. This is a likely quality, not a necessary one.

Secondly, rules may also have their first content of meaning overcome by contrary reasons, by means of a process of weighing reasons.[63] Moreover, that happens where rules relate with their exceptions. An exception may be provided for in the legal order itself, when judges shall weigh in the reasons and decide whether there are more reasons to apply the normative hypothesis of the rule or, in the contrary, to except it. For example, the legislation of a municipality may create a traffic rule according to which the speed limit within the urban area is 60 kph. If a vehicle if photographed by electronic devices at a higher speed than that, it will have to pay a fine. Such norm, given the classification analyzed herein, would be a rule and therefore would create an absolute obligation that does not involve weighing in the reasons for and against its use: if the vehicle is above the speed limit and the rule is valid, the penalty ought to be imposed. Still, the traffic department may not impose the fine on drivers, mostly taxi drivers, who can prove with an official report that at that time they were above the speed limit because they were taking a seriously wounded passenger to a hospital. In this case, even though the normative condition was effected, the judge evokes other reasons, based on other norms, to justify overruling that rule. The other reasons, considered superior to the reason to obey the rule, make up the grounds for overruling. That means, under the light of this topic, that the mode of application of the rule is not completely determined by a description of the behavior; rather, it depends on weighing in circumstances and arguments.

And the exception may not be provided for in the legal order, a situation where the judge will assess the importance of the reasons against the application of the rule, counterweighing the arguments for and against the creation of an exception in a concrete case. The case of statutory rape mentioned earlier is an example of this counterweighing. What matters is that the process through which *exceptions* are created is also a process of valuing reasons: because there is a contrary reason that axiologically outweighs the reason that serves as the grounds for the rule itself, one decides to create an exception. It is the same valuing process of arguments and counter-arguments, i.e., weighing.

As opposed to this understanding, one could say that the relation between rules and their express exceptions does not match the relation found between juxtaposing principles for two reasons. Firstly, one would say rules are interpreted whereas principles are weighed: the relation between a rule and its exceptions would be already set forth by the legal order, the judge having a duty to interpret it, whereas the solution to a collision of principles would not be previously defined, the judge having to weigh in reasons in order to build collision rules in a concrete case. Secondly, one would say the relation between rule and exception would not be a conflict since only one of them would be applied, either the rule or the exception, whereas the relation between two principles embodies a true conflict as both are applied although one is assigned greater weight.

These reasons are not convincing. Firstly, because interpreting and weighing can not be differed. Positively, the decision about the incidence of rules depends on assessing the reasons that support or not the inclusion of the concept of the fact into the concept the rule provides. If eventually one can say that the decision is merely coupling concepts, it can not be denied that the process that led these concepts to their final matching is at the level of weighing in reasons. Secondly, because it is not consistent with the statement that in the case of rules and their exceptions, only one norm is applied and in the case of juxtaposition of principles, both are. In fact, when judges assign a greater dimension of weight to one of the principles, they mean there are greater reasons to apply one principle and not another, which will not beam effects onto the actual case. The same happens in the case of an exception to a rule: judges decide there are greater reasons to apply the exception instead of the rule. That means that, where principles collide, the one with less weight may, in fact, not be applied; likewise, in the relation between rule and exception, either will not be applied. However one chooses to explain it, what matters is that in either case reasons and counter-reasons are counterweighed.

What one can say is something diverse. The relationship between general and exceptional rules and juxtaposing principles does not differ because of the weighing of reasons, but because of the extension of the judge's contribution in fixing this concrete relation and because of the weighing method: in the case of general and exceptional rules, normative conditions are partially shown by the preliminary meaning of the provision, thanks to the descriptive element of rules, and so judges have different and smaller leeway for analysis since they must delimit the normative content of the hypothesis if and while it is compatible with the goal that supports it; in the case of juxtaposing principles, because instead of descriptions there is the setting forth of a state of affairs to be reached, judges have more room for analysis as they must delimit the behavior required to realize or preserve the state of affairs.

Besides that, it ought to be pointed out that rules and principles do not relate in only one single way. In the case of relation between principles, where two principles lead to divergent goals, one ought to be chosen to the detriment of the other in order to solve the case. And, even if principles aim at the same goals, it is not impossible that they require different means to achieve them. In that case, one ought to be declared to take priority over the other and the other is consequently not applied in that concrete case. The solution is the same given to a conflict of rules that finds an exception, in which case both norms transcend the conflict and keep their validity.

In the case of relation between rules, even if the judge decides that one of the rules does not apply to the actual case, that does not mean it does not contribute at all to the decision.[64] Even when not applied, a rule can be a valuable opposition to the interpretation of the rule actually applicable, in which case not only it is not true that it does not contribute to decision-making, but actually the non-applied rule upholds the construction of the meaning of the applied rule by approximating and disjointing.

Thirdly, the rule weighing activity is found in the delimitation of semantically open normative hypotheses or legal-political concepts, such as the *Rule of Law*, *certainty of the Law*, *democracy*. In these cases, the judge must examine several reasons for and against the rule, or investigate a plethora of reasons to decide which elements comprise the legal-political concepts.[65] As hypothetically built provisions are the result of generalizations of the lawmaker, even the most precise formulation is imprecise because unpredicted situations may arise.[66] In this case, judges must analyze the goal of the rule and only from balancing of all circumstances of the cases will they be able to decide which factual element takes precedence in the definition of a normative goal.[67]

It is because of generalizations that some cases are not mentioned (*under-inclusiveness*) and others are wrongly included (*overinclusiveness*). Dogs are not allowed in restaurants because citizens usually have dogs and their dogs most usually annoy clients. Any dog is forbidden to enter. What if it is a newborn puppy wrapped in a blanket in her master's arms? A stuffed dog? A police dog used to find drugs or a suspected drug dealer? In these cases, the judge must assess the reason that justifies the rule in order to decide whether it applies, instead of simply focusing on the concept of "dog." If the reason that justifies the rule forbidding dogs to enter is the protection of the peace and safety of clients, the decision may be that the rule applies to the cases above. However, if one can go beyond the rule's hypothetical condition to the rule's purpose, the judge has the chance to forbid the entry of people who disturb clients' peace and quiet, such as crying babies, or to allow the entry of animals that do not risk clients' safety, such as a baby bear or even tame or anesthetized dogs.[68]

What matters is that the key point, rather than being the definition of the elements described by the normative hypothesis, is to know in which cases judges can refer to the rule's purpose in a way to understand the elements present in the hypothesis as mere pointers to the decision to be made and in which cases judges must abide by the elements described in the normative hypothesis in a way to understand them as the very reason to make a decision, regardless of any contrary reasons. Such decision depends on weighing the reasons that justify unconditional obedience to the rule, such as those linked to legal stability and foreseeability, and the reasons that justify putting the rule aside to favor an investigation of the grounds more or less close to the rule itself. This decision — that is the question — depends on careful weighing. Only by weighing reasons can one decide whether the judge is to abandon the elements described as operative facts of the rule while searching its foundations whenever they are incompatible.[69]

Fourthly, weighing rules takes place in deciding about the applicability of a legal precedent to the case under examination. As SUMMERS puts it, precedents are nor self-defining neither self-applying.[70] That means that deciding differently from set precedents depends on weighing reasons.

The fifth point is that rule weighing is found in the use of argumentative models such as *analogies* and *contrary arguments*, each supported by a different set of reasons that ought to be counterweighed.[71]

All these considerations show that reflecting on reasons is not a particularity of principles; rather, it is a general feature of any application of norms.[72] It is incorrect, therefore, to reason that principles, as opposed to rules, lack weighing and balancing (*abwägungsbedürftig*). Weighing is a part of both principles and rules, since any norm has a provisional quality that may be surpassed by reasons a judge sees as more relevant in a concrete case.[73] What varies is the kind of balancing.

Neither is it coherent to say that *only* principles *have* a dimension of weight. First of all, it is incorrect to stress that *only* principles have a dimension of weight. As the previous examples show, applying rules requires counterweighing reasons, whose importance the judge will assign (or coherently stress). The axiological dimension is not exclusive to principles, but an integral element of any legal rule, as proven by the application methods that relate, enhance or restrict the meaning of rules in regard to the values and goals they seek to protect. Extensive and restrictive interpretations are examples of such.[74]

Secondly, it is incorrect to stress that principles *have* a dimension of weight. A dimension of weight is not something that is *embodied* into a kind of norm. Norms do not regulate their own application. It is not, therefore, principles that have a *dimension of weight*: it is the reasons and goals which they refer to that a dimension of importance ought to be *assigned* to. Most principles do not say a word concerning the weight of reasons. It is decisions that assign principles a weight in regard to the circumstances of the actual cases. Such *dimension of weight* is not, therefore, an abstract quality of principles, but a quality of the reasons and goals which they refer to, whose actual importance the judge assigns. It is worth saying that the dimension of weight is not an empirical quality of principles that justifies a logical difference from rules, but rather a *result of the judge's valuation judgment.*[75]

Following are two examples that may show that it is judges who, given a case to examine, assign a dimension of weight to some elements to the detriment of others. The Brazilian Supreme Court analyzed a case where the Administration promised to lower the import tax percentage by decree, and then simply decided to raise it instead. Taxpayers, who had signed agreements in anticipation of the reduction promised, protested against the clearance of merchandise taxed at the raised percentage, and sued based on the principle of legal stability. The question before the Court could be solved in two ways: first, by assigning greater importance to the principle of legal stability in order to assure the citizen's trust in the acts of the government, and consequently bar the application of more burdensome tax rates onto those taxpayers who had signed agreements in expectancy of the promise to be fulfilled; second, by assigning importance only to the taxable event of importation, which occurs when the merchandise is cleared and therefore, the Administration having used its proper powers to raise the tax before the taxable event took place, there would have been no violation to a perfect legal act. The Court chose the second solution.[76] However, what does that mean to the question under discussion here? It means that an element's dimension of weight is not previously decided by the normative structure; rather, judges assign it in concrete cases. If the dimension of weight were an empirical quality of principles, the case under examination should have necessarily been solved on the grounds of the principle of legal stability and the assurance of protection to perfect legal acts; however, it was not. This is because it is not legal rules that determine absolutely which elements will be privileged to the detriment of others – it is judges that do so in concrete cases.

The Brazilian Supreme Court analyzed a case where the Official Diary, which should be published before the beginning of the year the tax should be paid according to a constitutional rule, was available in the evening of December 31, but subscribers were sent their copies only on January 2. Taxpayers rose against that, alleging that the principle of previous enactment had been violated, due to a constitutional norm that requires publication of acts before the end of the year as a means to ensure the predictability of government acts. At first sight, the case was to be decided by assigning importance to the principle of previous enactment and its two features: assuring predictability and requiring publication of new acts before the end of the year. The Court, however, instead of focusing on predictability or even on the requirement of prior publication, worked out a dissociation between publication and distribution which does not exist in the preliminary content of meaning of the provision under analysis. It thus understood that the fact that it was not *circulated* before the end of the year — here is the paradox — did not hinder knowledge of the content of the act, since the Official Diary was available to taxpayers before the end of the year.[77] However, what does that mean to the question under discussion here? It means, once again, that an element's dimension of weight is not previously decided by the normative structure; rather, judges assign it in concrete cases. If the dimension of weight were an empirical quality of principles, the case under examination should have necessarily been solved on the grounds of what scholars call the principle of previous enactment or on the grounds of the rule according to which a new act ought to be published before the beginning of the year when a tax becomes enforceable. That, however, did not happen. Again: it is not legal rules that determine absolutely which elements will be privileged to the detriment of others – it is judges that do so in concrete cases.

Ultimately, the examples mentioned here show that the mere classification as *principle* either in jurisprudence or in Case Law does not imply a consideration of weight in the sense of understanding a given provision as a value to be weighed against another. The Judiciary may neglect textual limitations or restrict the usual meaning of a provision. It can dissociate meanings in innovative ways. The connection between a norm and its preliminarily overlying value depends neither on the norm as such nor on features directly found in the provision from which it is construed as a hypothetical structure. Such connection depends both on the reasons judges use towards the norms they apply and on the circumstances assessed in the application process itself. That is to say, the dimension of weight does not relate to the norm but to the judge and to the case. Moreover, assigning weight depends on the *point of view* the observer chooses, and a norm may have more or less or even no weight at all for a decision, depending on the facts and their perspective. As HAGE correctly puts it, "*weight is case-related.*"[78] The structure of the norm does not predetermine how specific circumstances are considered, which *depends on how it is used.*[79]

A topic related to classifying principles by their dimension of weight is defining them as optimization commands. They are considered such because their content ought to be applied *to its maximum extent.*[80] However, it is not always so. In order to show it, one needs to identify what kinds of collisions between principles there are. They do not relate in one single way. Principles specify goals to be accomplished, but do not define beforehand the means to be chosen. When two principles collide, several situations may occur.

The first one of them refers to the fact that realizing a goal set forth by a principle always leads to the realization of a goal specified by another. That occurs in the case of interdependent principles. For example, the principle of legal stability sets forth stability as the ideal state of affairs to be achieved, and the principle of the Rule of Law also raises stability as a goal to be pursued. In this case, the principles do not limit each other, but reinforce each other. However, when the realization of a goal specified by a principle leads to the realization of a goal set forth by another, there is no duty of realization *to its maximum extent*, but only that which is strictly necessary to implement the goal specified by the other principle, i.e., *to its necessary extent*.

The second of them considers the possibility that the realization of a goal specified by a principle excludes the realization of a goal set forth by another. That occurs where principles point to alternate, excluding goals. For instance, while the principle of freedom of information allows the publication of news about people, the principle of protection of the private sphere prohibits publication of articles about people's private lives. That means that, where the realization of the goals created by one principle excludes the realization of a goal set forth by another, one does not find the reciprocal limitation and complementation of meaning mentioned above. Both ought to be applied in their entirety of meaning. The collision, however, can only be resolved by rejecting one of them.[81] Thus, this situation is similar to the case of the collision of rules.

The third situation refers to the fact that the realization of a goal specified by a principle may lead to the realization of only a part of the goal set forth by another. That occurs where principles partially juxtapose. In this case, reciprocal limitation and complementation of meaning exist on the juxtaposed portion.

Finally, the fourth situation refers to the possibility that realizing the goal set forth by a principle will not meddle with the realization of the goal created by another.[82] This is the case where principles promote ends extraneous to each other.

These reflections aim to show that the difference between principles and rules is not the fact that rules are applied *as a whole* and principles are applied *to their maximum extent*. Both species of norms ought to be applied in a way such that their ought-to-be content is fully realized. Both rules and principles have the same ought-to-be content.[83] The only distinction regards the behavior provision that results from their interpretation: principles do not directly order (therefore *prima facie*) which behavior to observe, they only set forth normatively relevant goals whose realization depends more intensely on an application act that shall have to find the behavior required to advance the goal; whereas rules depend less intensely on application acts in usual cases because the norm sets forth the behavior up front.

One also ought to remember that principles themselves are not orders of optimization. Actually, as AARNIO points out, such order consists of a normative proposition on principles and, as such, operates as a rule (hypothetical-conditional norm): it will be complied with or not. An order of optimization can not be *more or less* applied. Either one optimizes or not. The order of optimization, thus, regards the use of a principle: the content of a principle ought to be optimized while weighing takes place.[84] ALEXY himself now accepts the distinction between commands to optimize and commands to be optimized.[85]

The key point is not, therefore, a lack of weighing in applying rules, but the kind of weighing that is carried out and the way it ought to be validly founded, which is something different.

After critically examining the dominant conceptions regarding the definition of principles, a new definition can be proposed with basis on other elements. This is what is done next.

2.4. PROPOSAL TO DISTINGUISH PRINCIPLES AND RULES

2.4.1. Foundations

2.4.1.1. Justifying distinction Principles refer judges to values and different ways to produce results. It is common to say that values depend on markedly subjective assessments. They involve *a matter of taste*. Some people accept values that others reject. Some qualify as priority a value that others consider needless. That is to say, because they depend on subjective appraisal, values would be atheoretical, with no truth value, with no objective signification. As WRIGHT complements it, the understanding that values depend on subjective appraisal ought to be taken seriously.[86] Nevertheless, from that — and here commences our work — one does not derive neither the impossibility of finding behaviors that are mandatory due to the enactment of values nor an inability to distinguish between the rational and irrational applications of such values.

Concerning that matter, the ways principles are investigated surface. In this subject, it is easy to find two opposite ways of investigating legal principles. On one hand, principles can be analyzed in order to aggrandize the values they protect, though not examining which behaviors are indispensable to the realization of such values and which are the tools required to justify their application within controllable limits. In this case, the importance of principles is widely proclaimed, naming them the foundations or pillars of the legal order. More than that, practically nothing.

On the other hand, principles can be examined in order to privilege the exam of their structure, specially to find in it a rational procedure of justification that allows one not only to specify the behaviors required to realize the values they promote, but also to justify and control their application through a rational reconstruction of doctrinal statements and legal decisions. In this case, priority is given to the justifying character of principles and their rationally controlled use. The key point no longer is checking the values at stake, but becomes legitimating the criteria that allow the rational applications of these very values.[87] This is precisely the path this study follows.

2.4.1.2. Abstract distinction Distinguishing between normative categories, especially between principles and rules, serves two main goals. The first one is to *anticipate* the features of normative species so that when judges find them their task of interpreting and applying the Law may be eased. Secondly, as a consequence of that, such distinction aims to *lighten* the burden of argumentation by structuring it, since the classification of normative species allows lowering – though never eliminating – the need for justification by at least pointing to what is to be justified.[88]

It is clear that any classification of normative species will be inappropriate unless it either provides minimally safe criteria to anticipate normative characteristics or lowers the argumentative burden on judges.

A more attentive analysis of such distinctions between principles and rules shows that the criteria scholars use often manipulate elements that can only be assessed in concrete cases in order to interpret norms abstractly. In doing so, they elect abstract criteria of distinction that can not be – and often are not – confirmed in real application. Thus, classifications block the application of the Law instead of helping it. Instead of lightening the argumentative burden on the judge, they eliminate it.

Consequently, it is necessary to distinguish the preliminary level of abstract analysis of norms, usually called *prima facie* level of signification, and the conclusive level of concrete analysis of norms, usually called *all things considered* level of signification. This distinction helps verify why some criteria are more important for the first level, but inappropriate for the second, or vice-versa.

The criterion of the *hypothetical-conditional* aspect is inconsistent on both preliminary and conclusive levels. On the preliminary level, this criterion is inappropriate because any provision, even if not formulated hypothetically by the legislator, can be *reformulated* in a way to have a condition and a consequence. At the conclusive level, this criterion is inappropriate because, given the circumstances of real cases, judges must specify all aspects necessary to apply a certain norm by preparing elements the two introductory propositions of the syllogism and a consequence. In other words, given the circumstances of real cases, any norm can be formulated as a hypothesis. Every norm would be a rule.

Naturally, the *mode of application* criterion only makes sense at the conclusive level of signification. Indeed, if the distinction between principles and rules aims to facilitate the application of norms by anticipating normative features and easing the argumentative burden, this criterion becomes inconsistent because it can not be verified until the time of application. Thus, this criterion would only make sense if it allowed judges to anticipate safely the mode of application of a norm through the analysis of its structure. According to scholars, such structure is a conditional one. And when given a norm with a conditional structure, judges should immediately apply the normative consequence. That, however, can not be assured before analyzing all circumstances of a concrete case because, as seen, there may be justifying rules not predicted in abstract that overrule the reasons to apply the rule. That proves the catch of the *mode of application* criterion: it expects to show *beforehand* that which can only be shown *afterwards*.[89]

The *normative conflict* criterion is inconsistent at both preliminary and conclusive levels. At the preliminary level, it is correct to state that when two rules viewed as conditional structure norms conflict with each other, one of them ought to be declared void. Principles, viewed as norms that set forth goals to be accomplished, do not conflict directly. In abstract, they simply entangle. Regarding that, it is correct to say that rules and principles are different. Whereas a *total logical incompatibility* between rules can be conceived of analytically and abstractly with no regard for the particularities of concrete cases, a total abstract incompatibility between principles is inconceivable.[90]

In that sense, the *normative conflict* criterion is important, with some moderation. However, one can not categorically affirm principles as conflicting only in concrete cases, and rules in abstract ones.

On one side, there is an abstract conflict of principles, however partial. Even at the abstract level, one can find, at first sight, a scope far from the application of a principle by the simultaneous analysis of other principles. An examination of the relation between the principle of freedom of expression and that of protection of the private sphere reveals, even at an abstract level, that freedom of expression can not excessively hinder a citizen's private life. It is even possible to pre-select some cases of conflict.

On the other side, there are rules that coexist in abstract, but may be in conflict at a real level only. The case previously mentioned of a doctor's duties to tell the truth and to use all means to cure patients is one where they coexist harmonically in abstract, though they may conflict in a real case, e.g., where telling the truth may worsen a patient's condition.

What is left to know is the definition of principles and rules that encompasses this abstract distinction between the normative categories concerning their total logical incompatibility at an abstract level.

The axiological foundation criterion fits both levels of analysis. Axiological foundation is important at the preliminary and conclusive levels, although it is inappropriate to assign the primitive value to the norm and not to the reasons used by the judge after using it as a starting point.

A classification can not pretend to define normative species on a preliminary level in order to use elements that depend on considering all circumstances. Therefore, the *final mode of application* and the *normative conflict* criteria are inappropriate for an abstract classification, as they depend on elements that can only be verified upon consideration of all circumstances.

Their use as classification criteria of the normative species can, instead of working as a model that makes the application easier, act as an obstacle to the very construction of meaning of the norms, mostly those called rules, either because they may exclude the consideration of substantive justifying reasons for decisions foreign to the preliminary content of provisions or because they may limit the construction of axiological connections revealed among the elements of the normative system.

Even though rules usually feature an operative fact, automatic application and direct conflict with other rules, these features, rather than being necessary and sufficient to classify them as rules, are merely contingent. If this is so, another classification proposition ought to be adopted, as follows.

2.4.1.3. Heuristic distinction The proposition herein argued for can be called *heuristic*. As examined before, judges construe norms from provisions and their usual signification. This normative qualification depends on axiological connections that are nor embodied in the text neither belong to it; rather, they are construed by judges themselves. This is why the distinction between principles and rules is no longer a distinction with either empirical value supported by the very object of interpretation or with conclusive value which does not allow one to anticipate completely the normative signification and its acquisition method. Instead, it becomes a distinction that favors heuristic values, as it operates as a *model* or *temporary hypothesis* of study for an eventual reconstruction of normative values that does not ensure, however, any strictly deductive procedure of justification or decision about such contents.[91]

2.4.1.4. Distinction in inclusive alternatives The proposal supported here differs from the others because it accepts the coexistence of normative species due to a single provision. One or more provisions can be a reference to construe rules, principles and postulates. Instead of *exclusive alternatives* among normative species, in a way that the existence of one would exclude the existence of the others, a classification is proposed that houses *inclusive alternatives* in the sense that provisions may simultaneously generate more than one normative species. One or several provisions, or even their logical consequence, may have an immediate behavioral (rule), finalistic (principle) and/or methodical (postulate) *dimension*.

Let one examine the constitutional provision that requires the passing of an act, in its formal meaning, in order to allow the creation or increase of taxes. It is plausible to examine it as a rule, as a principle and as a postulate. As a *rule* because it conditions the validity of the creation or increase of taxes to the compliance with a certain procedure that leads to a specific source of norms — an Act. As a *principle* because it sets forth values of freedom and legal stability as due. And as a *postulate* because it binds interpretation and application to the acts and to the Law, previously excluding the use of parameters foreign to the legal order.

Let one examine the constitutional provision according to which all ought to be treated equally. It is plausible to apply it as a rule, as a principle, and as a postulate. As a *rule* because it prohibits the creation or increase of taxes that are not the same to all taxpayers. As a *principle* because it sets forth the value of equality as due. And as a *postulate* because it defines a legal duty of comparison (*Gebot der Vergleichung*) to be followed in interpreting and applying, previously excluding the differentiation criteria that are not set forth by the legal order itself.[92]

The previous reflections are important to show that the distinctions that argue for exclusive alternatives among normative species can be improved. Some examples will expose it. Some say irretroactivity *is* an objective rule.[93] Others say it is a principle.[94] Some say constitutional exemptions are rules.[95] Others say they are principles.[96] And so on, as the gentlemen LESSA describes as walking toward each other on an avenue where there was a statue with a shield made of silver on one side and gold on the other, who furiously grappled, each of them maintaining the shield was made up *only* of the metal each could see from his side.[97]

Thus, one must remember the fact that the provisions that are the starting point of normative construction can shoot forth a rule, if the judge prefers its behavioral aspect to the finality supporting it, as well as the foundations for a principle if the value aspect is given *autonomy* to reach behaviors inserted in other contexts. A provision, whose preliminary meaning sets forth a behavior to protect a value, in which case it would be classified as a rule, allows this value to be given autonomy to require other non-written behaviors required to realize it. For example, the meaning of the provision setting forth that taxes can only be created by acts can be classified as a rule, since the congressional procedure is expressly defined. That does not mean a different perspective can not examine that same behavior from its finalistic meaning of ensuring safety and stability to the taxpayers' activities. In this case, the definition of behavior indirectly preserves a value that is given autonomy and then demands the adoption of other behaviors independently. One can say that, when it conditioned the creation of taxes to the passing of an Act (article 150, I), the Federal Constitution defined a range of free initiatives that legislators must promote by allowing the behaviors necessary to promote it, such as allowing tax planning. In this case, the provision shoots forth a principle. These considerations show that a single provision can be the starting point to build rules and principles, as long as the defined behavior is analyzed from several perspectives, since one single provision can not be a principle and a rule at the same time and from the same perspective.

What is now proposed is exactly to overcome this normative species exclusive alternative focus in favor of a distinction based on the pluridimensional aspect of normative statements due to the arguments presented before.[98]

Besides proposing to overcome a dual model of *rule-principle* separation, based on the existence of condition and mode of application criteria and founded on exclusive alternatives, it also proposes the adoption of a three-part model of *rule-principle-postulate* distinction, which not only distinguishes rules from principles because of the duties they specify, the justification they require and the way they contribute to solve conflicts, but also adds the notion of postulates, defined as *methodical normative instruments*, i.e., categories that impose conditions to be observed in applying rules and principles, though different from them.[99] They will be mentioned again later on.

2.4.2. Distinction Criteria

2.4.2.1. Nature of described behavior Rules can be distinguished from principles regarding *the way they describe behaviors.* While *rules are immediate descriptive norms*, as they provide for obligations, permissions and prohibitions by describing the conduct to be followed, *principles are immediate finalistic* norms, as they provide for a state of affairs whose realization requires adopting some behaviors. Principles are norms whose up-front quality is exactly the definition of a legally relevant purpose, whereas the up-front quality of rules is the definition of behaviors.

Actually, principles set forth an ideal state of affairs to reach (*Idealzustand*), through which judges must inspect the appropriateness of the behavior chosen or to be chosen to protect such state of affairs. *State of affairs* can be defined as a situation defined by certain qualities. The state of affairs becomes a *purpose* when one aspires to obtain, enjoy or have the qualities in that given situation.[100] For example, the principle of the Rule of Law provides for states of affairs such as liability (of the State), foreseeability (of legislation), balance (of public and private interests), and protection (of individual rights), whose realization requires the adoption of certain conducts, such as the creation of actions aimed at placing liability on the government, publication of legislation prior to full enforcement, respect to the private sphere and fair treatment. So, when principles define purposes to be reached, they require the advancement of a state of affairs — legal assets — that imposes conducts required to preserve it or realize it. Therefore they are of a deontic-teleological character: *deontic* because they set forth reasons for the existence of obligations, permissions or prohibitions; *teleological* because obligations, permissions and prohibitions derive from the effects of a given behavior that preserve or advance some state of affairs.[101] Thus it is said that principles are *ought-to-be-norms*: their content regards an ideal state of affairs.[102]

Upon the previous reflections and the writings of WRIGHT, one can say that principles define a sort of *practical necessity*: they describe an ideal state of affairs that will be accomplished only if some behavior is adopted.[103]

As for rules, they can be defined as *mediate finalistic norms*, i.e., norms that set forth purposes indirectly, whose realization is aimed at with a more exact due behavior. Therefore, they depend less intensely on their relation with other norms and institutionally legitimate acts of interpretation in order to define the behavior due. In other words, rules are provisions whose up-front element is descriptive. Therefore they are of a deontic-deontological character: *deontic* because they set forth reasons for the existence of obligations, permissions or prohibitions; *deontological* because the obligations, permission and prohibitions derive from a norm that says "what" ought to be done.[104] Thus it is said that rules are *ought-to-be-norms*: their content directly regards actions.[105]

Both norms, however, can be analyzed from the behavioral as well as from the finalistic point of view: rules create the duty of adopting a *descriptively provided-for behavior*, and principles create the duty of adopting the *behavior required to realize* the state of affairs; rules describe a behavior to reach a certain purpose, whereas principles set forth the duty to realize or accomplish a state of affairs by adopting the necessary behaviors. Therefore, the distinction is centered on the nearness, whether mediate or immediate, of its relation with purposes to be reached and conducts to be adopted. That allows judges to know beforehand that principles as well as rules refer purposes and conducts: rules provide for conducts that advance the realization of due purposes whereas principles provide for purposes whose realization depends on required conducts.

It could be also made the distinction, within the category of principles, between those principles that command actions and those that command the maximization of states of affairs. This distinction, however, would not eliminate the definition of principles as goal norms; it would only make a specific distinction within a larger category, since the actions, commanded by these principles, are instrumental actions to promote states of affairs, such as equality or freedom. For this reason, fundamental rights are seen as principles too. Other rights, however, are, in the normative sense defended in this work, rules, not principles, when they are posited as preliminary descriptive norms.[106]

2.4.2.2. Nature of required justification Rules can be distinguished from principles regarding *the justification they require*. The interpretation and application of rules requires an assessment of the correspondence between the conceptual construction of facts and the conceptual construction of the norm and the finality supporting it, whereas the interpretation and application of principles requires an assessment of the correlation between the state of affairs placed as purpose and the effects derived from the conduct considered necessary.

This topic lets one see that the difference between normative categories is not centered on the mode of application, whether *all or nothing* or *more or less*, but on the *mode of justification* required to apply it. The option for this criterion does not focus on the final mode of application, whether absolute or relative, since it can only be confirmed eventually. This criterion investigates the justification required to apply it, which can be checked beforehand.

In the case of rules, because there is greater determination of behavior due to the descriptive or defining nature of the provisional statement, judges must argue in a way to justify an assessment of *correspondence* of the factual construction to the normative description and to the finality that supports it.[107] The expectation of a future state of affairs is immediately irrelevant. Therefore it is said that rules have a descriptive rather than a finalistic element.[108] The correspondence being easy to show, so is the argument burden lighter, because the normative description itself works as justification. If the conceptual construction of the fact, although matching the conceptual construction of the normative description, does not fit the purpose supporting it, or if it is overcome by other reasons, the argument burden is much heavier. Those are called hard cases. For instance, let us imagine legislation that forbids taxi and bus drivers to carry passengers with animals, specially dogs. If any vehicle is found to be transporting animals, its owner will be fined. Under the classifying model being examined, this norm would be a rule and thus create an absolute obligation: if the driver allows animals in the vehicle, and the rule is valid, the penalty ought to be imposed. However, the traffic department might not fine when passengers are blind and need a seeing-eye dog. Once again, the mode of application of the rule is not restricted by the definition of animal or dog. When the semantic content of a rule (e.g., prohibition of dogs in public transportation vehicles) and the justification supporting it (e.g., promoting traffic safety) diverge, judges end up analyzing reasons to adapt the content of the rule itself in exceptional and duly justifiable cases. In this case, an investigation of the rule's purpose allows not to apply a normative condition to cases that preliminarily would. That means, for what matters here, that the reason that generates the rule ought to be weighed against the significant reasons not to comply with it under certain circumstances, based on the purpose of the rule itself or other principles. To do that, however, a foundation is required that overcomes the importance of the reasons of authority that support unconditional compliance with the rule. Thus, the distinctive feature of rules is not their absolute mode of compliance. Their distinctive feature is the way they may not be applied fully, which is something else.

In the case of principles, the finalistic element substitutes for the descriptive element, so that judges must argue in a way to justify an assessment of *correlation* between the effects of the conduct to be adopted and the gradual realization of the required state of affairs. As it is not about showing correspondence, the argument burden is stable, and there are not easy and hard cases. Also, since there is no description of the behavior content, the interpretation of the normative content of principles depends more intensely on the exam of the issue. Truly, the principles of justification of Administration acts and morality of the Administration can not be construed without examining the cases where they were applied, or should have been applied but were not. There arises, then, a greater necessity to analyze paradigm cases in order to investigate the normative content of principles: it is necessary to investigate case whose solution may be a paradigm for similar cases, since they are based on values that can be generalized, as will be studied further on.[109]

What matters is that the distinction between rules and principles redirects to a judge's mixed knowledge and abilities regarding the object and the mode of justification of the interpretation decision.[110] Rules and principles diverge regarding their justification force and assessment object. Actually, because rules are immediate descriptive and mediate finalistic norms, an interpretation decision will be justified by assessing the accordance between the conceptual construction of facts and the conceptual construction of the norm. As principles are immediate finalistic and mediate behavior norms, the interpretation decision will be justified by assessing the effects of the conduct seen as the means necessary to promote a state of affairs which the norms set as the ideal to be reached.

It should be noticed that the present topic reveals that principles express the behavior required to realize them less emphatically. That does not mean that principles have an *apparent descriptive element*, as is the case with rules. Instead, it is stressed that principles, as they drive to a search for or preservation of an ideal state of affairs, eventually provide for the adoption of behaviors required to their realization, even though such behaviors are not described up front. In other words, principles do not immediately determine the object of behavior, but do determine its kind.

Due to that, one can also say that rules are *past regarding*, as they describe a factual situation known to the legislator, whereas principles are *future regarding*, as they set forth a state of affairs to be built.[111] This distinction, however, should be seen with some reservation. Surely, predicting facts yet to happen does consider past experience: it is not possible to assess which human behavior is appropriate to accomplish an ideal state of affairs without considering past behaviors and their relation with an achieved state of affairs. It is not correct, then, to state that only rules effect a valuation of past facts. One can affirm, however, that rules are norms whose nature is *primarily past regarding*, and principles are *primarily future regarding* norms. However, not more than that.

2.4.2.3. Amount of contribution to decision Rules can be distinguished from principles *regarding the way they contribute to the decision*. Principles are *primarily complementary* and *preliminarily partial* norms, as they cover only part of the aspects relevant to make a decision and thus expect not to generate a specific solution but to contribute to decision-making beside other reasons. For instance, the principle of consumer protection is not exclusive in the sense of providing for all and every consumer protection need, but only for those that can be combined with other provisions to promote other purposes, such as free initiative and ownership.

On the other hand, rules are *preliminarily decisive and including* norms, as they aspire to generate a specific solution for the conflicts of reasoning, despite their expectation of covering all relevant aspects to decision-making. For instance, the provision that denies political persons the jurisdiction to create taxes on books, newspapers and regular publications (article 150,

VI, d) predetermines which objects are preliminarily kept from taxation and, from this jurisdictional ban perspective, can be classified as a rule. In that sense, it intends to determine that only books, newspapers and regular publications can not be taxed, and previously rules out any doubts concerning other objects, such as pictures or statues, from its range of application. That would not happen if instead of predetermining which objects were exempt, the Federal Constitution only defined that all objects needed to manifest freedom of expression of thoughts and arts would be tax exempt. In this case, the solution regarding the conflict of reasons for and against the inclusion of certain objects in the scope of the norm would be open.

This topic emphasizes the *greater* interdependence between principles. Therefore their juxtaposition or entangling is emphasized. That happens precisely because principles set forth valuation guidelines to follow, but do not previously describe the appropriate behavior to accomplish goals. These valuation guidelines cross one another in several, not necessarily conflicting, directions.

Principles, therefore, *expect* to complement one another, as they cover only part of the aspects relevant to make a decision and thus expect not to generate a specific solution but to contribute to decision-making beside other reasons. *Therefore, principles are norms that expect to be complementary and partial.*

Rules, instead, expect termination as they expect to cover all aspects relevant to make a decision and thus aspire to generate a specific solution for the matter.[112] Meeting their conditions of applicability is the very reason for applying rules. Rules are, therefore, *preliminarily decisive and including* norms.

It should be pointed out that rules are only preliminarily decisive. That means they are not decisive as their conditions of applicability can be met though they are still not applicable because of some regard to exceptional conditions that overcome the reason that support the usual application of the rule. This phenomenon is called *defeasability*. Remember that when mentioning a more intense dependence of principles compared to other norms of the legal order, the topic excludes neither weighing in reasons nor even complementarity in the case of application of rules.

Finally, this topic emphasizes the creative collaboration of judges to make principles real. Because principles are purposes to accomplish, the appropriate behaviors to realize them and the very delimitation of their normative outlines depend – much more than rules do – on acts of the Judiciary, the Legislative and the Executive, without which principles do not acquire normativity.

2.4.2.4. *Comparison chart*

	Principles	Rules
Immediate Duty	promote an ideal state of affairs	adopt described behaviors
Mediate Duty	adopt necessary behaviors	remain faithful to underlying purpose and superior principles
Justification	correlation between effects of behaviors and the ideal state of affairs	correspondence between the concepts of norm and fact
Intention of deciding	complementary and partial	exclusive and overincluding

2.4.3. *Proposed Definition of Rules and Principles*

At this point, it is possible to reach conclusions and present definitions for rules and principles:

Rules are immediately descriptive, primarily past regarding norms which intend to decide and overinclude, whose application requires assessing correspondence, always centered on the purpose supporting it or on the principles axiologically overlying it, between the conceptual construction of the normative description and the conceptual construction of the facts.

Principles are immediately finalistic, primarily future regarding norms which intend to be complementary and partial, whose application requires assesssing the correlation between the state of affairs to be promoted and the effects of the conduct seen as necessary to its advancement.

As one sees, principles are immediate finalistic norms. They define a purpose to be met. As WEINBERGER puts it, a purpose is an idea that expresses a practical orientation. A component of the purpose is the definition of a *content* as expected. This explanation can only be understood regarding the pragmatic function of purposes: they represent a guiding, *directive function* (*richtungsgebende Funktion*) to determine behavior. The object of the purpose are the desired contents, which on their turn can be the accomplishment of an end-situation (e.g., traveling to a place), the realization of a situation or state (e.g., ensuring predictability), the pursuit of a continuing situation (e.g., preserving the well-being of people) or the quest for time-taking results (e.g., learning to speak German). The purpose does not necessarily have to represent any ending point (*Endzustand*), but only a desired content. Therefore it is said that purposes define an ideal state of affairs to accomplish, as a general form to frame the several contents of a purpose. The creation of the purpose is the starting point for the search for means. Means can be defined as conditions (objects, situations) that cause the gradual advancement of the purpose's content. Hence the notion that the means and purposes are correlated concepts.[113]

For instance, the principle of morality demands the *realization* or *preservation* of a state of affairs that manifests loyalty, seriousness, zeal, model behavior, good faith, sincerity and justification.[114] In order to realize this ideal state of affairs, some behaviors are necessary. In order to realize a state of loyalty and good faith, one needs to abide by what has been promised. In order to realize a state of seriousness, one needs to act for serious reasons. In order to realize a state of zeal, it is essential to cooperate with citizens and inform them of their rights and the way to protect them. In order to realize a state dominated by sincerity, it is indispensable to say the truth. In order to ensure justification, it is necessary to express the reason of acts. In short, the lack of these behaviors does not contribute to the existence of the state of affairs the norm sets as ideal, and therefore the purposes are not reached. Thus, the principle does not come true.

What matters is that if a state of affairs is to be sought and it is realized only through some behaviors, such behaviors become practical needs whose effects are needed to progressively advance the purpose. As WEINBERGER states it, a means-purpose relation leads to the transfer of intentions from purposes to means.[115] In other words, the enactment of principles implies the mandatory adoption of the behaviors required to realize it.

The reflections above show that principles are not only values which are accomplished on the basis of mere personal preferences. At the same time, they are more than that and something else. Principles create the duty of adopting behaviors required to realize a state of affairs or, conversely, the duty of effecting a state of affairs by adopting the behaviors it requires. This perspective of analysis signals that principles imply behaviors, even if indirectly and regressively. Moreover, this investigation reveals that principles may be indeterminate, but not absolutely. It may even be unsure regarding the *content* of the behavior to be adopted, but it is not regarding its *species*: whatever necessary to advance the purpose is due.

It is soon noticed that although principles relate to values, they can not be mistaken for those. Principles relate to values insofar as defining purposes implies a positive definition of a state of affairs to be promoted. However, principles withdraw from values because the latter are on a deontological plane and so define a mandatory adoption of behaviors required to the gradual advancement of a state of affairs, whereas values are on the axiological or merely teleological plane and so merely assign a positive attribute to a given element.[116]

Delimitation of the due behaviors, however, depends on the implementation of a few conditions. In fact, how can one know which conditions make up the ideal state of affairs sought and which behaviors are necessary to accomplish it? Some methodic guidelines help find the answers to these questions.[117]

This work defines rules as immediately descriptive, primarily retrospective norms that intend to be decisive and overarching; whose application requires an assessment of *correspondence* between the conceptual construction of the normative description and the conceptual construction of the facts. Thus, a question arises as to know whether this definition is compatible with the various kinds of rules, notably the jurisdiction rules (those that assign a person the power to pass given acts) and the defining rules (those that assign a normative meaning to some acts or facts). Such questioning arises because these norms do not describe a behavior, but only assign a power or a legal effect. The answer is yes: these rules also embody the general elements that define rules: a descriptive character and the requirement to assess the correspondence between the factual construction and the normative description. This can be shown from the examination of several kinds of rules. Naturally, there are several criteria to classify rules, which we will not do here. Such would not be pertinent as long as the discussion herein concerns only the general definition of principles and rules.

With that purpose, rules can be divided into two large groups: behavioral rules and enacting rules.[118] Behavioral rules describe behaviors as mandatory, allowed, or forbidden. Enacting rules assign legal effects to certain acts, facts, or situations, and can be rebuilt from the following provisions:

1) *Provisions related to assigning jurisdiction*: assign a person a certain power to perform a certain act. For example, the provision according to which the parliament has the power to enact laws.
2) *Provisions related to exercising jurisdiction*: regulate the procedure to exercise a given jurisdiction, or competence. For example, the provision according to which the creation of statutes must follow parliamentary proceedings.
3) *Provisions related to substantive delimitation of jurisdiction*: circumscribe the substantive scope of jurisdiction. For example, the provision according to which the creation of taxes is limited to the Legislative Power.
4) *Provisions related to the exclusiveness of jurisdiction*: determine which exclusive normative sources are able to regulate certain subjects. For example, the provision according to which only a statute in its strict sense may create taxes.
5) *Provisions related to the substantive delimitation of jurisdiction*: delimit the content of jurisdiction. For example, the provision according to which the Law ought to treat all citizens equally, without any form of discrimination.

Given this range of normative provisions, one asks once again: do all of them set forth behavior norms and require the judge to examine the *correspondence* between the factual construction and the normative description and then to its supporting goal? In the general terms proposed herein, the answer is yes.

In the case of provisions that assign jurisdiction, the judge may simultaneously rebuilt three norms: a rule of permissive conduct, allowing a subject to exercise a given activity; a rule of forbidden conduct, preventing other subjects from exercising the same activity; and a defining rule, defining a given source as able to produce certain effects.

In the case of provisions related to the exercise of jurisdiction, the judge may simultaneously rebuilt two norms: a rule of mandatory conduct, compelling a given subject to adopt a certain behavior in order to exercise a power validly; and a defining rule, defining as normative only those sources that were created according to a certain procedure.

In the case of provisions related to the substantive delimitation of jurisdiction, the judge may simultaneously rebuilt two norms: a rule of mandatory conduct, compelling one to exercise power only over some subject-matters; and a rule of forbidden conduct, preventing someone from exercising power over other subject-matters.

In the case of provisions related to exclusive jurisdiction, the judge may simultaneously rebuilt three norms: a rule of permissive conduct, assigning a subject the power to create a certain normative source; a rule of forbidden conduct, preventing the subject from creating a different normative source; and a second rule of forbidden conduct, preventing the subject from delegating to another subject the power to create a given source.

Finally, in the case of provisions related to the substantive delimitation of jurisdiction, the judge may simultaneously rebuilt three norms: a rule of mandatory conduct, compelling a subject to include some given content in the normative act to be created; a rule of forbidden conduct, preventing the subject from including different content in the normative act; and a rule of permissive conduct, assigning the subject the power to exercise a certain act.

Within the scope of this work, what matters is that in each of these cases norms describe objects (subjects, conducts, matters, sources, legal effects, contents) and require the recipient to choose a generally set behavior, and require the judge to examine the correspondence between the adopted conduct and the normative description of that object. Such correspondence, in a broad sense, can refer both to a requirement for conformity (assessing whether the adopted conduct is deduced from the normative provision) and also to a requirement of compatibility (assessing whether the adopted behavior does not counter the normative description).

The descriptive character of the object – and the conduct it refers – and the requirement of correspondence are absent in the case of principles. This is because principles do not describe an object in a broad sense (subjects, conducts, matters, sources, legal effects, contents). Rather, they set forth an ideal state of affairs that ought to be *promoted* and therefore do not require the judge to examine the correspondence, but the *correlation* between the state of affairs to be promoted and the effects arising from the conduct regarded as necessary to its promotion. In sum, despite the several kinds of rules, one can still state that, in general, they opposed principles under the following criteria.

Firstly, rules are different from principles because of their *normative descriptive nature*: while rules describe definite objects (subjects, conducts, matters, sources, legal effects, contents), principles describe an ideal state of affairs to be promoted.

Secondly, rules are different from principles because of the *kind of justification* that they require in order to be applied: rules require an examination of the correspondence between the normative description and the acts performed or facts occurred, whereas principles require an assessment of the positive correlation between the effects of the adopted conduct and the state of affairs that should be promoted.

Thirdly, rules are different from principles because of the *kind of contribution* to the solution of the problem: while rules intend to be decisive, as their goal is to offer a temporary solution for a known or expected problem, principles intend to be complementary, as they serve as reasons to be coupled with other towards the solution of a problem.

2.4.4. Consequences of the Inconsistent Use of the Weak Distinction Between Rules and Principles

Roughly speaking, there are two jurisprudence mainstreams to define principles.[119] The first one states that principles are norms of high level of abstraction (aimed at an uncertain number of situations) and generality (aimed at an uncertain number of people), and because of that their application calls for a high degree of subjectivity from the judge, as opposed to rules, which show little or no degree of abstraction (aimed at a (nearly) certain number of situations) and generality (aimed at a (nearly) certain number of people), and because of that their application calls for little or no subjectivity from the judge. This is the classical theory of Public Law, which has made its way from studies of Administrative Law and finally into works on Constitutional Law. Hence comes the statement that principles are the foundation, the main pillars, or the values of the legal order, upon which its effects radiate.

The basis of this distinction, depending on the degree to which it is defended, is the degree of uncertainty of normative species: because they are more fluid, principles allow for greater valuation mobility, whereas rules, believed to be determined, eliminate or significantly decrease judges' freedom of appreciation. As one may see, it is a weak distinction: principles and rules have the same properties, though at different degrees – whereas principles are more indeterminate, rules are less.

The distinction based on the degrees of abstraction and generality is quite disseminated in Tax Law jurisprudence. Such dissemination has triggered two inconsistencies: one is semantic, and the other is syntactic.

The semantic inconsistency concerns the inappropriateness of defining a principle based on its high degree of abstraction and generality. This criterion of distinction between normative species has been harshly criticized. Perhaps the main criticism has been that every norm, as long as language is used to express it, is indeterminate to some extent and thus it is pointless to distinguish normative species by something common to all of them – indeterminateness. Given that the application of norms requires a vast process of balancing reasons and facts, the apparent determinateness may disappear as well as the supposed indeterminateness may transform into clarity in a concrete case. Not to mention that the application of norms covers many others aspects than merely semantics.

The same is true of the value content. Because it is aimed to a certain goal, every norm is the means to the realization of values, and rules are the means for the realization of at least two values: the formal value of stability, since rules intend decisiveness that principles do not have; and a specific substantive value, since each rule has an underlying goal. Therefore, it is pointless to base a distinction between normative species in their value content, since it brings them together instead of setting them apart.

It should be noted that the distinction between normative species on their indeterminateness and language value content may eventually recede the latent indeterminateness of rules and their concealed value content, by changing them into second class norms because of their would-be determinateness and supposed value neutrality. Moreover: such distinction may create the belief that interpreters do not have any freedom to configure the semantic and value content of rules, when in reality every legal norm, including rules, only has its meaning content and underlying goal defined by means of a process of weighing and balancing. On the other hand, this distinction criterion may ultimately lead to an overvaluation of principles, as if the application of any rule could be brought up to a level of pure principles without justifications or explanations.

Semantic inconsistency has consequences on the syntactic plane: many who define principles as norms with specific properties (high degree of abstraction and generality) insist in calling principles norms that do not have such properties. But if a principle is defined as a norm of high degree of abstraction and generality, which therefore requires application with a high degree of subjectivity, one may ask: can the normative prescription that allows a deduction of the industrialized products tax equivalent to the operative amount of previous operations be considered a principle? Can the normative prescription that requires publication of the act that creates or increases a tax by the end of the fiscal period prior to its collection be considered a principle? Can the normative prescription that prohibits the legislator from taxing events that occurred before the enactment of the law be considered a principle? Can the normative prescription that prohibits the creation of taxes based on certain events be considered a principle? Can the prohibition of illicit evidence be considered a principle? Of course not. Where are the properties of high degree of abstraction and generality in the case of the norm that requires previous publication in order to create or increase a tax, for instance? They are not present anywhere. The norm that requires publication of the act that creates or increases a tax by the end of the fiscal period prior to collections is a rule, for example.[120]

Such internal contradiction of the jurisprudence is not a simple matter of naming, which is secondary. It would be about names if it did not bring about two fundamental problems: one, if they did not link such norms to properties they do not actually have – high degree of generality and abstraction; two, if they did not link such norms to a specific consequence for their application – high degree of subjectivity. As long as these are the characteristics, the theory falls into a contradiction, and – much worse – it legitimates flexible applications of norms that the Constitution, given the normatization technique it used, designed to be less flexible.

2.4.5. Consequences of the Inconsistent Use of the Strong Distinction Between Rules and Principles

The second jurisprudence mainstream, led by the studies of DWORKIN and ALEXY, states that principles are norms that are applied by weighing and balancing with others and that may be realized to several degrees, as opposed to rules, which definitely set forth a hypothesis that is mandatory, allowed or forbidden, and therefore requires application by coupling fact and rule hypotheses. This is the modern theory of Public Law, which has made its way from studies of Philosophy and General Theory of Law, and finally into works of Constitutional Law. This concept originates the statements that principles are different from rules relative to how they are applied and how antinomies among them are solved. The difference concerning application is as follows: whereas rules set forth final commandments and are applied by coupling fact and hypotheses, wherein the judge ought to compare the factual concept and the hypothetical concept of the norm and then, if both match, apply the consequence, principles set forth contingent duties and are applied by weighing and balancing, as the judge will have to assign a weight to the principles according to the concrete case. The difference concerning the solution of antinomies is as follows: whereas the conflict of rules is abstract, mandatory and imports the declaration of invalidity of one of them unless an exception is created, the conflict of principles only occurs in concrete cases, is contingent, and does not import the declaration of invalidity of any of them. Rather, it imports the creation of a rule of prevalence given certain circumstances found only on the plane of efficacy of the norms.

The foundation of this distinction lies in the normative structure: because principles institute commandments that are defeasible when confronted against other principles, they can be counterweighed, whereas rules eliminate or sensibly decrease the judge's freedom of appreciation because they establish supposedly definite duties. As one can see, this is a strong distinction: principles and rules do not have the same properties; they have different qualities. Whereas rules establish definite standards (which are not defeasible by contrary reasons) and are applied by coupling (an examination of the correspondence between the normative concept and the factual substantive concept), principles establish provisional standards (which are defeasible by contrary reasons) and are applied by weighing (actual counterbalancing of colliding reasons by assigning greater weight to one of them); whereas the conflict between rules is abstract (conceivable in itself on an abstract plane), necessary (it cannot be avoided unless an exception is created) and located on the plane of validity (the conflict is solved by declaring one of the rules as not valid), the antinomy of principles is concrete (it only happens in certain concrete circumstances), contingent (may or may not happen), and located on the plane of efficacy (both principles remain valid after the conflict).

This normative structure-based distinction has been recently put forward in Tax Law jurisprudence. As a consequence, it has also caused two inconsistencies: one is semantic and the other is syntactic.

The semantic inconsistency concerns the inappropriateness of defining a principle with basis on the final models of application and antinomy solution. This distinction between normative species has suffered a lot of criticism. The application model, weighing or coupling, is not appropriate to differentiate them since every legal norm is applied by means of balancing. Rules do follow such standard, as they are subject to both internal and external weighing: internal because the reconstruction of the semantic content of the hypothesis and its underlying goal depends on a confrontation between the several reasons for each interpretation alternative (example: definition of the meaning of "book" in order to determine a substantive aspect of the rule of constitutional tax exemption); and external when two rules are harmonic in theory, but conflict before a concrete case without causing any one of the two rules to be declared as non-valid (example: a rule that sets forth a preliminary injunction to avoid irreparable damage and another rule that prohibits such injunction if it brings expenses to the Public Treasury). It is therefore inappropriate to distinguish between normative species with basis on properties both species share – counterability and defeasibility.

The same occurs concerning the solution of antinomies. Although the conflict of rules is usually solved by declaring one of them as not valid, that does not happen every time. One can identify conflicts of rules that have the same characteristics of the conflicts between principles – concrete, contingent, and on the plane of efficacy. Thus, it is not appropriate to base a distinction between normative species on the way they solve antinomies if in some cases that will bring them together instead of setting them apart.

It should also be noted that a distinction between normative species based on their application and solution of antinomies may also lead to a trivialization of the operation of rules, changing them into norms that are applied automatically and without their needed weighing of reasons. Moreover, such distinction makes one believe that rules are not defeasible, when in reality every legal norm, including rules, sets forth provisional values, as shown by the cases of rules cast aside because of extraordinary reasons with basis on the postulate of reasonableness. On the other hand, such criteria of distinction, if not beside precise application and argumentation criteria, may indirectly lead to an arbitrary use of principles, which could be downplayed or overstated according to specific interests.

The semantic inconsistency also has consequences on the syntactic plane: those who define principles as norms with specific properties (application by counterbalancing and conflict solved by ranking against other principles) insist in calling principles norms that do not have such properties. But if a principle is defined as a norm that can be realized to several degrees depending on the principle with which it actually conflicts, which is why it requires an application that assigns it a weigh, one may ask: can the rule of non-cumulativeness, as a norm that allows deducting from the tax amount due the amount paid in the previous economic cycle, be qualified as a principle and be downplayed because of other principles? Can the requirement of previous enactment, as a commandment that requires publication of the act that creates or increases a tax by the end of the fiscal year prior to its collection, be considered a principle and be restricted in a concrete case? Can the norm of irretroactivity, which forbids tax norms from applying to events occurred before the publication of the acts that create or increase taxes, be considered a principle and downplayed in the face of contrary reasons? Can the norm of tax exemption, as a norm that preempts certain events or people from being taxed, be considered a principle and have its semantic content invalidated? Can the norm that prohibits the use of illicit evidence be considered a principle and become subject to free malleability? Of course not. Where are the referred properties of lack of hypothetical structure, of possible realization in several degrees according to the restrictions of other principles? They are not present. These norms are rules for this stream of thought as well.

Again, it must be pointed out that this internal contradiction of the jurisprudence of the strong distinction is not about a simple matter of naming. It would be about names if it did not bring about one fundamental problem: assigning a specific consequence for the application of norms – susceptibility of more flexible defeasibility due to contrary reasons. As long as these are the characteristics of principles, the theory falls into a contradiction, and – much worse – it legitimates the easy restriction of a norm which, given the chosen normatization technique, the Constitution designed to be less flexible.

A related matter is the widely publicized jurisprudential concept that not following a principle is worse than not following a rule. In general, it is the other way around: not following a rule is worse than not following a principle. This is so because rules have an intended decisiveness that principles do not: whereas rules intend to supply a provisional solution for a conflict of interests the Legislative knows of or expects, principles only offer complementary reasons to solve a conflict that may happen in the future.

Another related matter is to know which norm ought to prevail if there is a conflict between a principle and a rule on the same hierarchal level (constitutional rule vs. constitutional principle). Based on the already mentioned traditional concept, jurisprudence usually states that the principle ought to prevail. However, this should not be so. If that were accepted, the collision of the rule of tax exemption for books and the principle of freedom of expression of thought and culture would have to assign priority to the principle, including – this would be one of the consequences – the exemption of works of art! And if there were a conflict between the rule of jurisdiction to create social contribution taxes over revenues and the principles of social solidarity and universal financing of social security, principles should prevail, even – this would be one of the results – for the sake of justifying taxation even if the amounts collected by companies did not match the concept of revenue! Alas, this is not acceptable.

As one can see, both classifications – weak and strong – are not void of effects, as they bring consequences for the judges: for the former, application will have a high degree of subjectivity because the norm is highly open; for the second, counterbalancing will assign a weight to principles that collide in a concrete case. Because there are significant consequences regarding the application of norms, both the mistaken concept (the concept of principle connotes properties that normative language cannot connote) and the inappropriate naming of a norm (calling a norm principle although it does not have the properties the concept of principle connotes) cause an undesired normative result: downplaying or overstating the application of a norm that ought to be applied more exactly. It backfires: in order to make a norm more effective, jurisprudence calls it a principle, but in doing so it legitimates its downplaying and weakens its efficacy; in order to increase their value, jurisprudence calls some norms principles, but in doing so it eliminates the chances of valuing rules, thus diminishing them; in order to fight formalism, jurisprudence redirects the application of the legal order to principles, but in doing it without pointing to minimally objective criteria for their application, it increases unfairness by intensifying arbitrariness; in order to put forward a progressive and effective application of the legal order, jurisprudence refers to the norms considered more important as principles, but in doing it with the implication that principles require application to be intensely subjective or downplaying due to contrary reasons, it sets the ground for conservativeness to be legitimated.[121]

2.4.6. Guidelines to Analyze Principles

Whereas principles are defined as finalistic norms which require the delimitation of an ideal state of affairs to be sought through the behavior necessary to accomplish it, the following steps are proposed to investigate principles.[122]

1st - Specifying purposes to their maximum extent: the less specific a purpose, the less its realization can be controlled

The beginning of progressive delimitation of purposes is to build relations between the constitutional norms themselves in a way to structure a chain of argumentation centered on the aggregating principles. Reading the Federal Constitution with a focus on delimiting purposes is indispensable. For instance, instead of assigning the promotion of public health to the Administration without delimiting what it means in each context, one needs to demonstrate that public health means, in the context under analysis and according to some provisions of the Federal Constitution, the duty to offer vaccine "X" to block epidemic "Y". *In short, specific purposes must substitute for vague purposes.*

In concrete terms, it means: (a) to read the Federal Constitution, and pay specific attention to the provisions related to the principle under analysis; (b) to list provisions according to fundamental principles; (c) to try to make purposes less vague by analyzing constitutional norms that may directly or indirectly restrict the scope of application of the principle.

2nd - Researching leading cases that may start up such process of clarification of the conditions that make up the ideal state of affairs to be achieved through the behaviors necessary to its realization.

Leading cases are those whose solution may be seen as exemplary, meaning a solution that models the solution of such other cases because of the generalization ability of its content of value. For instance, instead of merely stating that the Administration must rule its activity by standards of morality, one needs to show that in some cases the duty of morality has been defined as the duty to effect expectations by fulfilling promises made beforehand or as the duty to effect statutory goals by adopting serious and justified behaviors. *In short, vague purposes ought to be replaced with the behaviors necessary to achieve them.*

In concrete terms, it means: (a) to investigate the precedents, mainly those of higher courts, to find leading cases; (b) to investigate the chosen decisions in their entirety; (c) to observe, in each case, which behaviors were considered necessary to realize the principle under analysis.

3rd Examining these cases for similarities that may form a set of cases that gravitate towards the solution for the same central problem.

When investigating some cases (the case of an employee who acted according to a memo circulated within a financial institution, which later did not want to abide by it; the case of a student who was granted transfer from one university into another and, years later, saw such transfer voided due to a formality defect; and the case of a company who was granted a tax benefit year after year to further a business venture and then had it voided for formality irregularities), one can notice that the court decision in all of them was centered on the problem of protecting the legitimate expectation the Administration created for citizens' legal sphere, mostly when such expectation was confirmed in facts over several years. In other words, *the mere listing of isolated cases must give way to an investigation of the legal problem they contain and values to preserve for their solution.*

In concrete terms, it means: (a) to analyze the presence of a common problem that brings different cases closer; (b) to check the values leading to the solution of the problem.

4th - Looking for the presence of criteria that enable the delimitation of which legal goods make up the ideal state of affairs and which behaviors are considered necessary to achieve it.

Some cases investigated in the analysis of the principle of morality may reveal, on one hand, the duty to realize loyalty, and on the other the need to adopt serious, rational and clarifying behaviors to bring such value to life. *In other words, the achievement of a concrete purpose substitutes for the search for an ideal.*

In concrete terms, it means: (a) to analyze the presence of criteria that let one assert, in other cases as well, which behaviors are necessary to realize a principle; (b) to disclose the criteria that may be used and the foundations to adopt it.

5th - Trailing the way backwards: having found the state of affairs and the behavior required to promote it, it becomes necessary to look for other cases that should have been decided according to the principle under analysis.

The second step in examining principles, as mentioned, relates with the investigation of precedents, mostly those of Higher Courts, in order to identify which behaviors were considered necessary to realize the principle under analysis in each leading case.

There are cases, however, in which a given principle is used though not expressly referred to. In other cases, even though the promotion of a purpose is mandatory, such principle is not used as justification. Because of that, after unveiling the typical applications of the principle under analysis, it is necessary to research anew, not to search for the principle as a keyword, but to search for the state of affairs and behaviors considered necessary to achieve it.

In other words, it means (a) to redo the search for precedents with other keywords; (b) to analyze critically the decisions found, rebuilding them according to the principle under examination so as to illustrate their disuse.

These steps show that the path to be trailed is long. Every effort it requires has a precise purpose: to overcome the mere veneration of values and move towards a progressive and rational delimitation of the behaviors required to achieve the purposes presented by the Federal Constitution.

2.4.7. Example of the Principle of Morality

The use of these guidelines can be exemplified with the exam of the principle of morality, however summarized. The provision used as a starting point for the construction of the principle of morality is presented in article 37 of the Federal Constitution, which includes morality as one of the fundamental principles of administrative acts. The Federal Constitution does not simply name morality; rather, it assigns morality great importance in several provisions. A short organization of the preliminary meaning of these provisions shows that the Federal Constitution is concerned with behavior standards in several ways.

Firstly, *it defines fundamental values*, such as dignity, work, free initiative (article 1), justice (article 3), equality (article 5, caput), freedom, property and safety (article 5, caput), stability of relation (article 5, caput and XXXVI). The specification of these values implies not only the duty to consider them in acts of the Administration, but also the prohibition to restrain them without a plausible justification.

Secondly, *it defines an objective, impersonal style of administration*, based on the principles of the Rule of Law (article 1), separation of powers (article 2), statutory legality and impersonality (articles 5 and 37). The creation of an objective manner of acting implies that acts under legal protection are preferred to those carried out arbitrarily.

Thirdly, *it creates mechanisms to protect the rights of the citizens* by making justice accessible to everyone (article 5, XXXV), prohibiting the presentation of illegally obtained evidence (article 5, LVI), controlling acts of the Administration through writs of mandamus and popular legal actions, even against acts harmful to morality (article 5, LXIX and LXXIII), and by voiding acts of dishonest administration (article 37, § 4). The creation of mechanisms of defense makes it possible to annul acts of the Administration that fall short of the standard of conduct legally chosen.

Fourthly, *it creates requisites to enter a public career*, such as the requirement of public contests (article 37, II); the prohibition of the accumulation of positions (article 37, XVI) and self-promotion (article 37, XXI, §1); the need to show moral capacity or untainted reputation to take office as a Justice in the Court of Audits (article 73), the Supreme Court (article 101), the Superior Court of Justice (article 104), the Superior Court of Elections (article 119), the Circuit Court of Elections (article 120); the requirement of moral capacity to request Brazilian citizenship (article 12); and the prohibition of reelection as a violation of morality (article 14). The acclamation of these conditions to enter a public career implies a choice for seriousness and reputation as qualities of public persons.

Fifthly, *it creates several mechanisms to control the acts of the Administration*, including the administrative acts legitimacy controls of the Courts of Audits (article 70).

The organization of the preliminary meaning of these provisions as a whole shows that the Federal Constitution defined such a strict behavior standard to enter a public career and exercise it that, in case seriousness, justification and purpose inexist, acts can be reviewed by internal and external mechanisms of control.

In order to detail this rigid behavior standard better, one must find leading cases that clarify the meaning of the seriousness, justification and purpose that delimit the desired morality. Following are some.

A public authority allowed time to run out on a public contest that would fill in positions for District Court Judges, having sworn in only thirty-three of the fifty applicants who had passed it, and then ordered publication for a new contest with the same purpose. Questioned for the reasons for non-acting, this authority made infer that time was not extended for personal reasons. In this case, intentional inertia, twist on imperative norms, unreasoned malice, lack of exemplary stance and absence of serious reasons were evidenced. Such behaviors are incompatible with the seriousness and truthfulness necessary to advance administrative morality.[123]

A person requests a transfer from a federal university to another, which is granted, causing the person to effect the transfer and start attending the course for a long time. Later on, the administrative authority verified that a formality was not complied with, which is the reason why it is claimed to void all previous acts that allowed the transfer. In this case, the non-fulfillment of a certain promise was evidenced, and an expectation created by the Administration itself was struck. Such behaviors are incompatible with the loyalty and good faith necessary to advance administrative morality.[124]

It can be seen that the principle of morality demands serious, loyal, rational and clarifying behaviors, even if not provided for by statute. Then, these are violations of the principle of morality, to behave without objective parameters with basis on an agent's individual will, and to act without regard for the expectation created towards the Administration.

Having analyzed principles and rules, we must now examine how their effects take place. Let us move on to the efficacy of principles and rules.

2.4.8. Efficacy of Principles

2.4.8.1. Internal efficacy

2.4.8.1.1. Content

Norms act upon other norms of the same legal system, specifying their sense and value. Principles, which are norms oriented to immediate goals, set forth an ideal state of affairs to be sought concerning other norms of the same system, notably the rules. Therefore, principles are important to the understanding of the meaning of the rules. For instance, the rules of constitutional tax exemption are properly understood if interpreted according to its overlying principles, such as is the case of the interpretation of the reciprocal exemption (each federative member cannot impose any tax on the other) based off the federation principle. Such aptitude to produce effects on different levels and functions can be called efficacy function.[125]

2.4.8.1.2. Direct internal efficacy

Principles act upon other norms directly and indirectly. One can observe *direct efficacy* when action does not interact nor interrelates with another (sub)principle or rule. Within the scope of their aptitude to produce effects, norms play different roles, some of which are predominant and require specific analysis.

On the direct efficacy plane, principles play an *integrative function,* as they justify the aggregation of elements not provided in subprinciples or rules. Even if an element inherent to the sought purpose is not set forth, the principle will still ensure it. For instance, if there is no express rule setting forth a defense opportunity or defining when a party can manifest its position in a lawsuit – however necessary these are – these should be ensured with direct basis on the principle of due process of law. Another example: if there is no express rule ensuring the protection of a potential right – however necessary to implement a state of trust and stability for the citizen – it should be protected with direct basis on the principle of legal stability (or the principle of protection of legitimate expectations). In these cases, some principles will act directly.

2.4.8.1.3. Indirect internal efficacy

One can observe *indirect efficacy* when the action interacts or interrelates with another (sub)principle or rule. On the indirect efficacy plane, principles play several roles.

Firstly, concerning the more ample norms (superprinciples or above-principles, i.e., principles situated above other principles), principles play a *defining function*, as they limit, with further specification, the more ample command set forth by the axiologically superior superprinciple. For example, the subprinciples of protection of trust and objective good faith should specify the scope of the superprinciple of legal stability in more concrete situations.

Morevoer, and now concerning norms of more strict scope, (super)principles play an *interpretive function*, as they are used to construe norms from expressly normative texts, both restricting or broadening its meanings. For example, the principle of due process of law requires interpretation of the rules that ensure the citation and defense in a way such as to ensure effective protection of citizens' interests. Although several subelements of the principle of due process of law are already embedded in the legal order, the principle of due process of law is not redundant because it allows each one to be "reread" or "interpreted accordingly" to it. In the case of the principle of the Rule of Law, the same happens: although several of its subelements are embedded in the legal order (e.g., separation of powers, previous legal provisions, individual rights), it is not unnecessary, as each element should be interpreted with the higher purpose of ensuring the legality and responsibility of the acts of the State. Such rationale qualifies principles as *objective value decisions with an explanatory function* (*objektive Wertentscheidung mit erläuternder Funktion*) in the cases that guide the interpretations of legal or constitutional norms.

Finally, principles play a *blocking function*, as they remove express elements that are incompatible with the general state of affairs to be promoted. For example, if there is a rule setting forth a term for defense, but the time is not enough to ensure effective protection of a citizen's rights, then a proper term should be ensured due to the blocking efficacy of the due process of law.

Superprinciples such as the rule of law, legal stability, human dignity and due process of law play important functions, even in the – rather common – case of those whose subprinciples the legal order already sets forth. As principles, superprinciples play typical principle functions (interpretive and blocking), but because they superimpose over other principles (therefore the term "superprinciple"), they do not play either the integrative function (which implies direct action, whereas superprinciples act indirectly) or the defining function (because this function, though indirect, implies more specialization, whereas superprinciples act in order to broaden and not to specify). In fact, the function superprinciples distinctively play is the *reordering function*, as they allow the interaction of several elements which make up an ideal state of affairs to be sought. For example, the superprinciple of the due process of law allows the interrelation of the subprinciples of extensive defense and opposition with the rules of summons, subpoenas, appointed judge and admissible evidence, in a way such that each element, given the relation it engenders with the others because of the superprinciple, is given a new meaning, diverse from that it would have if it were construed in isolation.

2.4.8.2. *External efficacy*

2.4.8.2.1. Content

However, legal norms do not act solely upon the understanding of other norms. They act upon the understanding of the facts and evidence themselves. Indeed, whenever a legal norm is applied, one must decide which, from all facts that took place, are pertinent (*pertinence exam*), and which, from all viewpoints, are appropriate to interpret the facts (*valuation exam*).[126]

At this point, in comes the notion of *external efficacy*: legal norms are fundamental to the interpretation of the facts themselves. One does not interpret the norm and then the fact, but rather interprets the fact according to the norm and the norm according to the fact, simultaneously.[127] What matters most here is to emphasize the external efficacy of principles: as they indirectly create values by creating an ideal state of affairs to be sought, they indirectly supply a parameter for the examination of pertinence and valuation. For example, the principle of legal stability sets forth an ideal foreseeability of the State's action, a measurability of obligations, a continuity and stability of the relations between the Government and the citizens.

2.4.8.2.2. Objective external efficacy

2.4.8.2.2.1. Selective efficacy

The interpretation of facts should then privilege a *selection* of all the facts that could affect the foreseeability, measurability, continuity and stability. For example, if a principle protects foreseeability, the judge cannot disconsider facts that prove a citizen was caught off guard in the exercise of his or her economic activities.

This is the *selective efficacy of principles*, based on the fact that the judge does not interpret raw facts, but builds upon facts. Facts are built through the mediation of the interpreter's speech. The very existence of the fact does not depend on the experience, but on the argumentation.[128] They are not ready made.[129] In other words: broadly, it is the judges themselves who decide which facts pertain to the solution of a controversy *as they develop their cognition*. In order to decide which facts are pertinent, interpreters should use the axiological parameters provided by the constitutional principles so as to select all the events centered on legally protected interests. An event will be pertinent when its factual representation is required to the identification of a constitutionally protected legal interest. Indeed, principles protect certain legal interests (actions, states or situations that ought to be sought or maintained) and let one determine which factual elements are relevant. Thus, it is a retrooperative procedure, since it is the principles that determine which facts are pertinent through an *axiological revisitation* of the factual material. The Law does not choose the facts, but it offers criteria that can then be applied to the events for building the facts.[130]

2.4.8.2.2.2. Argumentative efficacy

After selecting the pertinent fact, one must valuate them in order to *emphasize* the points of view conducive to the emphasis of aspects of these facts that eventually protect such legal interests. Within a given category of facts, the interpreter must seek the angle or viewpoint which constitutional principles support.[131] One must sort of define the situation based on legal objectives.[132] This is the *valuation efficacy function*.

There is also the *argumentative efficacy*. Because constitutional principles protect some legal estate and interests, the greater the direct or indirect effect on the preservation or realization of these interests, the greater ought to be the justification for this restriction on the part of the State (*postulate of the increasing justifiability*). As such, principles also have efficacy which is not only interpretive, but also argumentative: The State, if adopting measures that restrict some principle it ought to promote, shall present justifications for such restriction, to an extent as significant as that of the restriction.

2.4.8.2.2.2.1. Direct

Firstly, principles describe a state of affairs being pursued without a previous definition of the means whose adoption will produce the effects that will contribute to promote it. This key characteristic of principles was well noted by ALEXANDER and SHERWIN: "*In the case of a* standard, *the role of the Lex (or Super Lex) is to identify ends and values to be pursued while saying very little about the means of pursuing them.*"[133]

A norm that protects the freedom of speech, without defining how such freedom will be pursued, is a principle. That is so because, although it defines the goal to be pursued, it leaves the judge free to choose the means to do so.

Secondly, since principles only point to goals to be pursued, they enact part of the controversy and require the complementation of other principles for their application. This is the very reason the decision ought to be made by a quantitative weighing of the principles actually colliding. This feature was also noted by ALEXANDER and SHERWIN: "*In other words, the rule-maker is not attempting a complete settlement of controversy.*"[134] That happens because principles do not bring up a solution for the conflict of interests that may arise during their application, as they leave open the choice of means to promote them.

2.4.8.2.2.2.2. Indirect

Given their complementary aspect, principles, when applied, include the reasons one considered during the conflict.

Instead of facing prohibitions or restrictions in the activity of investigating the moral reasons behind norms, the judge will be free to weigh these reasons directly against one another.

Finally, as principles do not previously set the means of government action, they do not bind judges to an operation of matching the concepts of normative hypothesis and the case facts.

Instead, judges have the duty of weighing and balancing the conflicting principles regarding the concrete case, and find themselves the means that are appropriate, necessary and proportional to the realization of the goals set forth by the enactment of the principles.

2.4.8.2.3. Subjective external efficacy

Concerning the subjects the efficacy of principles affects, it should be noted that the legal principles act as subjective rights when they prohibit the intervention of the State in freedom rights, also qualified as *defense or resistance function* (*Abwehrfunktion*).

Principles also direct one to take measures that protect freedom rights, also known as *protective function* (*Schutzfunktion*). The duty of the State is not only to respect fundamental rights, but also to promote them through the adoption of measures that accomplish them in the best possible way.

2.4.9. Efficacy of Rules

2.4.9.1. Internal efficacy

2.4.9.1.1. Direct internal efficacy

As seen previously, rules have a *preliminarily decisive efficacy*, as they hope to offer a temporary solution to a given conflict of interests the Legislative has already detected. Therefore, they preempt the free weighing of principles and demand evidence that the State acted within the scope of its substantive jurisdiction.

2.4.9.1.2. Indirect internal efficacy

In relation to the more ample norms (principles), rules play a *defining function* (realization), as they delimit the behavior to be adopted in order to realize the goals the principles set forth. For instance, the legal rules of parliamentary procedure will specify, in more concrete situations, the scope of the democratic principle.

As mentioned previously, rules have more rigidity, as they are not overcome unless there are sufficiently strong reasons for such, either in the underlying goal of the rule or in its superior principles. This is why the defeasability of rules is only possible given extraordinary reasons to do so, the analysis of it being subject to the postulate of reasonableness, discussed further on. The word "entrenched" illustrates the obstacles rules create to their overcoming, much greater than those a principle poses. This is why, in case a principle and a rule on the same hierarchal level are in actual conflict, the rule should prevail, not the principle, due to the decisive function that qualifies the former. The rule is a sort of preliminary parliamentary decision regarding a conflict of interests, and should thus prevail when conflicting with an immediately complementary norm, as is the case of principles. Therefrom arises the *entrenchment efficacy function* of the rules.

In respect to this, one should point out the importance of revisiting the broadly publicized Public Law concept that violating a principle is much more serious than violating a rule because it would mean the violation of several commands and the subversion of fundamental values of the legal system.[135] Such concept is based on two premises: first, that a principle is worth more than a rule, when in fact they have different functions and goals; second, that a rule does not incorporate values, when in fact it crystallizes them. Besides that, the underlying idea of reproachability should be reexamined. As rules have an immediate descriptive character, their commands are much more intelligible than those of principles, whose immediate character is only the accomplishment of a state of affairs. In that sense, it is more reproachable to not comply with that which "one knew" he or she was supposed to comply with. The greater the previous degree of knowledge of duty, the greater is the reproachability of the transgression. On the other hand, it is more reproachable to violate the defining realization of values in a rule than those values pending a definition and complementation, as is the case of principles. As one sees, reproachability – that is what this work advocates – must be linked to the degree of knowledge of the command, first, and then to the degree of intended decisiveness. In the case of rules, the degree of knowledge of the duties is much greater than that in the case of principles, given the immediately descriptive and behavioral character of rules. Notice that knowledge of the content of the norms to be complied with is valued by the legal order itself through the principles of statutory legality and publicity. Noncompliance with a known duty is more serious than noncompliance with a norm whose content is pending further complementation. Or, to put it simply: noncompliance with a rule is graver than noncompliance with a principle. In the case of rules, the degree of intended decisiveness is much greater than that of principles, because a rule is a sort of solution for a conflict of interest that the Legislative knows or anticipates. One should notice that the respect to previous decisions is also valued by the legal order through the protection of acquired rights, the perfect legal acts and the judicial decisions. Noncompliance with what has been decided previously is more serious than noncompliance with a norm whose function is to complement other reasons in forming a future decision. Or, to put it simply: noncompliance with a rule is graver than noncompliance with a principle. If not so, because absent another argument to modify the equation, the burden of overcoming a rule is greater than that required to overcome a principle.[136] Contrary to general belief, therefore, the legislative option for rules reinforces their preliminary standing.

Hence, such considerations reveal the *different functionality* of principles and rules: rules are norms intended to solve conflicts between legal goods and interests, and convey *a strong prima facie character and more rigid overcoming* (i.e., rule-generated reasons, when opposed to other reasons, require a greater argumentation burden to overcome); principles are norms intended to complement, and convey *a weak prima facie character and more flexible overcoming* (i.e., principle-generated reasons, when opposed to other reasons, require a smaller argumentation burden to overcome).

A related question is that of conflict between norms, mostly between principles and rules. One usually argues that, when a principle and a rule collide, the former prevails. The concept this work advances goes a different path. First of all, one should study whether norms are hierarchically different: in the conflict of a constitutional norm and an infraconstitutional norm, the higher norm should prevail, regardless of its type being a principle or a rule. For example, in a conflict between a constitutional rule and a statutory principle, the former should prevail; and if there is a conflict between a statutory rule and a constitutional principle, the latter should prevail. That means the prevalence does not depend on the norm type, but on the hierarchy. However, when both norms are on the same hierarchal level, and a true conflict occurs, the rule should take precedence. For example, when there is a conflict between the principle of freedom of expression of opinions and the rule of tax exemption for books, the tax exemption rule should be given precedence. Otherwise, one could argue for the exemption of works of art, since these can also be used to express opinions. One should point out that, in such case, it would make more sense to refer to a *substantive connection* between the norms than to refer to a conflict. Instead of opposition, there is complementation. There is a reciprocal justification between the rule and the principle: the interpretation of the rules depends on the simultaneous interpretation of the principles, and vice versa.

Apparently, the only plausible case of assigning "prevalence" to a constitutional principle to the detriment of a constitutional rule would be upon substantiation of an extraordinary reason that hindered application of the rule. For example, a conflict between the principle of human dignity and the rule that ranks the priority of government payments. In this case, however, the rule would not be applied because of an extraordinary reason that hinders its application, given the postulate of reasonableness. Strictly speaking, though, it would be more correct to claim there is no conflict, since there would not be two applicable norms, but a single one, differently from what occurs in a true conflict, when two applicable norms do so remain to the end of the conflict, leaving the interpreter with a choice between the two in a concrete case.

Even though the Constitution sets forth conceptual barriers when it uses specific expressions, one may still think that a constitutional order that embraces rules as well as principles could allow one of two circumstances: either the prevalence of principles over rules, with the former acting directly where the latter does not, or an enlargement of the concept a rule sets forth due to an indirect action of principles in its interpretation. Both cases, though conceptually discernible, have the same legal effect: the creation of a new restriction with no express assignment of power by any rule. Neither of these, however, is acceptable.

This is so because rules must prevail in a horizontal conflict between rules and principles, unlike one might suppose from the description of principles as the most important norms of the legal order. Indeed, rules have an efficacy that principles do not, as has been studied. The constitutional provision of principles or institutions correlated to such jurisdiction rules does not void the previous conclusion, as the provision of principles and institutions does not bind the adoption of behaviors required to their realization, *unless the legal order predefines such means by jurisdiction rules.*

Although it has not been directly expressed, this reasoning is that of the Brazilian Supreme Court in the Direct Motion for Unconstitutionality (ADIN) 815, in which a member of the Federation (the State of Rio Grande do Sul) claimed that a constitutional rule was unconstitutional. The rule concerned the proportion of State representatives in the National Congress, and was confronted with the federation principle. The Court decided to dismiss the motion, considering the pleading as legally impossible, and it reasoned that it could not use a principle to outweigh the defining realization chosen by the Original Constitutional Power by means of constitutional rules. Thus, it reasoned that the Framers ordained the federation principle, but did so in the terms of the rule set forth in article 45, with the restrictions determined therein. From this decision, one learns that one Power is not allowed to revisit the "balancing" carried out by the Original Constitutional Framers. This is so much so that the Opinion states, on page 347, that the principle of equality is limited by the Constitution itself in article 5, item I, or that the democratic principle is limited by the Constitution itself in article 1 (*"as ordained by this Constitution"*). Likewise, an opinion was endorsed from the General Attorney which stated that *"the Plaintiff's argument about the possibility of the existence of unconstitutional provisions due to norms seen as having higher hierarchy is not acceptable."* (p. 318) Finally, the Court decided that the Constitutional Power is free to set the limits of a constitutional principle, since *"those who are free to set a principle are also free to set its exception."* (p. 325). Such exceptions are created by means of rules. One can say that the Supreme Court, in other words, decided that whoever is applying the principle, whether the Judiciary or the Legislative, cannot outweigh a rule by a constitutional principle because of the defining and final characteristic of rules.

The Brazilian Supreme Court used the same reasoning to analyze the possibility of solving the conflict between the constitutional warranties against the use of illicit evidence and the public interest of punishment. Instead of weighing and balancing the individual rights ruled by the Constitution against the colliding public interest, the Supreme Court decided that it is not its role to weigh and balance anew what the Constitution already has decided by setting forth a rule. A good example is the opinion of Justice Sepúlveda Pertence: "Though I do not ignore the soundness of different thinking, I resist accepting that one may oppose the constitutional warranty against the use of illicit evidence to the public interest in punishing crimes in general, or some specific crimes, with the ultimate intention of making the latter prevail over the former in the name of the principle of proportionality. This is because, in this case, the Constitution itself has balanced the opposing values and chosen – to the detriment of crime persecution, if so be the case – the fundamental values of human dignity, which are protected by the prohibition of illicit evidence."[137]

Similar understanding was made by the Brazilian Supreme Court through the decision about the enlargement of a social tax. In this case, two positions were confronted: on the one side and based on different ways of argumentation, some Judges sustained that social principles, such as social solidarity or universal financing of social welfare, could justify the extension or the defeasibility of the constitutional competence rule that provided the State the power to tax only a specific fact in order to cover also another different fact; on the other side, some Judges, based on different argumentative techniques, argued that the constitutional competence rules, precisely because they establish conceptual limits, could not be extended or defeated by constitutional principles. Not considering here the details of the case, the Supreme Court gave more importance to the constitutional competence rules when they conflict with constitutional principles.[138]

In sum, it is inadmissible to outbalance a constitutional rule due to a principle, or to broaden it beyond a set semantic limit, because the rule itself is the constitutional solution for a given conflict of interests. This is especially true, considering that the Federal Constitution does not have only one principle that may outbalance or broaden a rule; rather, it has several principles, not all pointing to the same direction. An interpretation that focuses exclusively on one principle disregards the constitutional order as a whole. The same is true of interpretation that under the pretext of preserving supposedly prevalent values ends up outbalancing the constitutional rules that have realized these very values.

2.4.9.2. External efficacy

2.4.9.2.1. Selective efficacy

Rules have a preponderantly external efficacy of determining conduct (*behavioral rules, Handlungssätze*) and assigning a given subject the jurisdiction to perform a legal act concerning a given subject (*competence norms* or *power conferring rules, Kompetenzregel*).[139] Rules select facts, concepts and conducts.

2.4.9.2.2. Argumentative efficacy

2.4.9.2.2.1. Direct

Firstly, rules describe the behavior to be followed or the portion of power to be exercised by its addressee. A norm that, instead of being limited to protecting health, goes further and defines how such protection is to be pursued, is a rule. This is so because the subject does not have an open choice of means; on the contrary, the rule defines specific means.

The choice of specific means of government action by the enactment of a rule does not leave the Legislative or the Executive free to choose other means, however better these might seem. When there is a rule, then, the moral conflict that might have arisen in case the rule had not been enacted will no longer arise, given the decisive effect of the enacted rule. Thus say ALEXANDER and SHERWIN: "*Rules are to settle what ought to be done by supplanting moral considerations.*"[140] Likewise are the words of GOTTLIEB: "*Rules are designed to allocate decision-making authority, as well as to control discretion. With rules, instead of an indeterminate opaque box, judges have a set of instructions that can be described reasonably well and can be applied in a sufficiently clear way that one can often check on the correctness of a particular judge's use of them*".[141]

Secondly, rules, having previously weighed all relevant aspects of the conflict of principles, expect to set forth a decision for such conflict. In this manner, they generate, as mentioned earlier, a specific solution for the conflict of reasoning. In other words, once a rule has been enacted to set forth a specific decision for a conflict of principles, the Legislative and the Executive Powers are not allowed to weigh the conflicting principles again and make another decision. Therefore, it is said that rules are indifferent (or at least resistant) to the reasons they aim to harmonize. Said ALEXANDER and SHERWIN: "*They are opaque to the moral principles they are supposed to effectuate.*"[142]

Indeed, rules have the task of creating a solution for a conflict, thus preventing the shunned controversy of moral values from arising anew when applied. The Constitution framers carry out a previous weighing and balancing that shuns an eventual horizontal weighing.

2.4.9.2.2.2. Indirect

Rules, given their decisive character, exclude reasons that would otherwise be considered had the technique of enactment by rules not been chosen. In other words, had there been no rule, the judge would be free to decide the matter by considering other reasons; however, as there is a rule, such reasons are excluded by the reasons the rule imposes. Therefore, it is said that rules set forth second order reasons that block the action of first order reasons.[143] In the words of RAZ: "*First, exclusionary reasons exclude by kind and not by weight. They may exclude all the reasons of a certain kind (such as, considerations of economic welfare), including very weighty reasons, while not excluding even trivial considerations belonging to another kind (such as, considerations of honour). (...) Their impact is not to change the balance of reasons but to exclude action on the balance of reasons.*"[144]

What matters is that all those reasons that would be considered cannot be considered because of the enacted rule, which becomes the very reason of the decision. Thus wrote SCHAUER: "*Rules* block *consideration of the full array of reasons that bear upon a particular decision in two different ways. First, they exclude from consideration reasons that might have been available had the decisionmaker not been constrained by a rule. Second, the rule itself becomes a reason for action, or a reason for decision.*"[145]

Such blocking ability in constitutional interpretation has been well perceived by PILDES, who wrote as follows: "*The 'excluded reasons' approach to constitutional law entails a distinct method approach of judicial decision making. When courts apply this approach, explicitly or, more commonly, implicitly, they do not balance individual rights against state interests. Judicial rhetoric aside, the process is not the purportedly quantitative one of assigning weights to these incommensurable entities. Defining excluded reasons is instead a qualitative task, one that requires courts to evaluate the justifications for public action against the principles that give different spheres their unique normative structure.*"[146]

These characteristics of rules have unequaled importance for constitutional interpretation, so long as they modify the very process of constitutional conflict resolution, which jurisprudents not always bear in mind, as PILDES notes: "*It is surprising to discover how many constitutional conflicts are most clearly resolved through this reasoning process. Many cases that seem to require balancing of individual rights against state interests turn out instead to require, more simply, the definition of excluded reasons. The best account of these cases is that courts today, like their counterparts in the late nineteenth century, are primarily interpreting the constitutional logic that defines the boundaries between separate spheres of political authority. When this method is at work, the problem of balancing is dissolved.*"[147]

In such cases, the legitimacy of the power is not discovered by means of qualitative balancing of the state interest and the individual interest, in the sense that one will admit a greater restriction to the individual right to the extent that the pursued state goal has greater importance; instead, the legitimacy of the power is investigated by means of a qualitative analysis that studies the structure of the power that is assigned by a rule. Thus states PILDES, when referring to the qualitative or structural method of rule interpretation compared to the qualitative or balancing method of principle interpretation: "*The difference between these alternative rights paradigms – one individualistic, the other structural – has significant implications for constitutional law, including the apparent problem of balancing. Under the individualistic conception of rights, courts 'balance' the weight of individualized harms and the strength of legitimate state interests. Under the structural conception, courts evaluate the reasons for state action in different spheres. The structural approach self-consciously recognizes that courts are not engaged in a seemingly quantitative exercise, but in the interpretative task of defining principles of state action that the Constitution permits in various spheres. The individualistic conception reasons 'from the inside out' – from an assessment of the burdens on individuals to an examination of the strength of the state's interests. The structural conception of rights focuses directly on a question external to the individuals involved – the legitimate scope of state authority.*"[148]

Such considerations have the utmost relevance for constitutional interpretation because, in the presence of a specific rule concerning the controversy, interpretation is no longer based on free, horizontal balancing, and rather becomes centered on the internal balancing of the rule hypothesis itself. PILDES wrote in that wise: "*If we focus instead on the central role of 'excluded reasons,' constitutional law would become less a matter of defining boundaries on political authority in different areas.*"[149]

Lastly, one ought to draw attention to the fact that the previously examined descriptive aspect of rules brings forth consequences regarding the analysis of the language defined by the Constitution. As mentioned, the choice of rules sets forth jurisdiction scopes that are very different from those that might exist in the case of the establishment of principles: whereas in the latter case the Legislative may choose the means to promote goals, in the former case it is previously bound to the constitutionally chosen means. That is so because rules are immediately descriptive of conducts or assignments of power for the adoption of conducts, and judges are to apply the rule whose concept ultimately corresponds to the concept of the facts.

Constitutional concepts can be determined in two ways. In the direct way, the Constitution expressly states the meanings of the concepts it uses. Indirectly, the constitutional framers use expressions whose meanings were already conveyed in concepts created by the non-constitutional legislators at the time of the promulgation of the Constitution, and then choose to use them in the constitutional order. In any case, the Constitution defines limits the congressional legislator cannot cross while it is in force.

That language is largely undetermined is true. From the fact that it is undetermined, though, one cannot derive that it does not have nucleuses of determination, or that it is completely undetermined and therefore unnecessary. [150] In other words, even if undetermined, that does not mean it does not have nucleuses of signification or that it cannot be determined by usage or even by the very system in which it is integrated.

2.4.9.3. Defeasability of rules

2.4.9.3.1. Argument of obedience to the rules

One may sustain that rules ought to be followed simply because they are rules. It is the old idea of MONTAIGNE, according to which laws ought to be followed because they are laws, not because they are fair.[151] From this angle, the argument of obedience to the rules revolves around the idea of authority. This argument obviously creates great resistance to rules, especially when one knows that their application will cause unfair results in specific situations. However, one can sustain that rules ought to be followed not only because they are rules, but also because obedience to them, in itself, is positive for several reasons.

Firstly, as rules have the role of pre-deciding the means of exercising power, they shun the uncertainty that would arise had this choice not been made. It is precisely in order to avoid the arising of a moral conflict and to shun the uncertainty caused by a lack of resolution of such conflict that the Legislative Power chooses to enact a rule. Thus state ALEXANDER and SHERWIN: "*The purpose of having Lex promulgate rules to settle questions about how moral principles apply in concrete situations is to eliminate the controversy and uncertainty and their associated moral costs*".[152]

Secondly, besides shunning controversy and uncertainty, the choice for rules aims to eliminate or reduce the arbitrariness that may potentially arise in the case of direct application of moral values. This characteristic was noted by SCHAUER, when he analyzes the importance of the resolution in rules as a means to restrict discretionary, unrestricted government acts: "*In sum, it is clearly true that rules get in the way, but this need not always be considered a bad thing. It may be a liability to get in the way of the wise decisionmakers who sensitively consider all of the relevant factors as they accurately pursue the good. However, it may be an asset to restrict misguided, incompetent, wicked, power-hungry, or simply mistaken decisionmakers whose own sense of the good might diverge from that of the system they serve.*"[153]

Likewise, SHEPPARD stresses the importance of rules in reducing potential arbitrariness in the manipulation of principles: "*In the hands of an honest merchant, the balance is an implement for fine comparisons of honest value. Used by a corrupt merchant, however, the balance is a tool for deceit, a scale in which truth is weighed against gold or* pudding *against praise.*"[154] All that because, upon leaving the question open for the Judiciary or Executive to decide, according to equitable reasoning they may find more appropriate, one runs the risk of arbitrariness, as finalizes SCHAUER: "*Perhaps most important in explaining the legalization of equity, however, is the recurring concern with the potentially arbitrary and nonpredictable nature of the equitable power, regardless of who exercises it.*"[155]

Thirdly, the choice of rules ultimately avoids problems of coordination, deliberation, and discovery. In this sense, ALEXANDER and SHERWIN clarify: "*The determinateness requirement refers to the moral functions that the rules are meant to serve: coordination, expertise, and efficiency. The indeterminateness of the moral principles regarding how they apply to particular cases is what produces the controversy and uncertainty that results in lack of coordination, costly deliberation, and mistaken (inexpert) discovery*".[156] Indeed, the absence of rules would cause an immense lack of coordination among people, each defending personal points of view as prevalent. The absence of solutions, even if they could be modified by extraordinary reasons, would result in excessive costs since each case would have to be solved separately, with specific authority and justification. Moreover, in the absence of rules citizens would feel legitimized to create solutions, even in areas that require specialized technical knowledge, which would jeopardize the safety of people and the efficiency of decisions.

In sum, these ideas show that rules ought not to be followed only because they are rules and an authority passed them. They ought to be obeyed because on one hand obedience to them is morally good, and on the other hand they produce effects towards values the legal order itself encourages, such as safety, peace, and equality. Unlike the current exaltation of principles might lead one to think, rules are not second class norms. Much on the contrary, rules play a very important function of predictable, efficient and usually equitable solutions of social conflicts.

2.4.9.3.2. Defeasability conditions

2.4.9.3.2.1. Introduction

In the chapter concerning rules, it has been shown that rules also involve values and require balancing, and that they may be outweighed under exceptional circumstances. This topic has shown that under normal circumstances rules ought to be obeyed because obedience to them promotes predictable, efficient and usually equitable solutions of social conflicts. In general, rules are not absolute, but they are not easily outweighed, either. Now what is left to study are the conditions required to outweigh them.

The model proposed hereafter has two characteristics. First: it is two-dimensional, as it is simultaneously substantive and procedural. It is substantive because it requires certain contents in order to allow the outbalancing of rules. And it is procedural because it requires the observation of certain formal requirements in order to allow the outbalancing of rules. Second: it is criterion-oriented, as it does not seek only to analyze whether rules may be outweighed, but when and in the presence of which conditions they may be outweighed.

2.4.9.3.2.2. Substantive requirements

As rules are instruments of predictable, efficient and usually equitable solutions of conflicts, outweighing them will be as much easier the less unpredictability, inefficiency and inequality they bring forth. The study of two different examples may illustrate the degree of resistance to rules.

A rule mandated that eligibility for a program of simplified payments of federal taxes was conditional to not importing foreign products. Participants could not import under penalty of exclusion from the program. That was the normative hypothesis. The actual case concerns a small sofa manufacturer that imported once, and was therefore immediately excluded from the program. However, all it imported was only four legs for a single sofa, only once. Upon appeal, the exclusion was reversed because the rule was not reasonably applied. In this case, the rule hypothesis did occur, but the corresponding consequence was not applied (exclusion from the special tax payment system) because the goal that justified the rule (encouraging national production by small companies) was not threatened by not behaving according to the rule.

In this case, accepting the individual decision (permission to import, when the rule forbids it) does not harm the promotion of the goal underlying the rule (encouraging national production by small companies). On the contrary, a single, individual permission for the company to continue enjoying the tax benefit would favor national production, as the import would be used exactly to better manufacture in the country. Moreover, accepting an individual decision that did not match the general hypothesis would not endanger legal stability; on the contrary, it was indifferent, since the specific circumstances (importing a few parts of a product) would hardly be repeated or alleged by other taxpayers, and it would be hard to prove its unique character. That means, in other words, that acceptance of the individual case does not harm the verification of the two values inherent to the rule: the formal value of stability is not restricted because the case is hardly repeatable by other taxpayers, and the substantive value of encouraging national production would not be reduced since the behavior would actually help promote it. The attempt to do justice to a case by outweighing a rule would not affect the promotion of justice for the most part of cases. And the contrary – not outweighing the rule – would do more harm than good.

The same thing does not occur in a different kind of situation. A rule stated that filing a certain appeal depended on appending readable copies of the appealed sentence and documents that proved the matter had been discussed on the records of the lawsuit. The actual case concerns an appeal that was filed without copies of the petition and the sentence that denied the request. Unhappy with the denial, the appellant filed an appeal, alleging a violation of the principle of universal jurisdiction and denouncing the excessive formality in the interpretation of the rule that demanded the copies and documents. The Appellate Court, however, sustained the original decision, and argued that the appellant ought to file appeals with all documents necessary to understanding the matter under discussion, since such requirement does not serve the purpose of pointless formality, but that of assuring stability to the parties and safeguarding the due process of law.[157] In this case, the hypothesis put forth in the rule did occur and the corresponding consequence, notwithstanding harm to one of the parties, was applied (the appeal was not admitted) because not adopting the behavior in the rule would have harmed the promotion of the goal it aimed to promote (legal stability).

In this second case, accepting the individual decision (admitting the appeal in spite of the lack of the legally required documentation) would harm the promotion of the goal underlying the rule (stability and safety of parties). On the contrary, accepting this only appeal would drastically harm the stability of parties, who would not know which rules to follow, and the judicial decision itself, since the matter under discussion would not have been precisely delimited. Moreover, accepting an individual decision not in accordance with the general rule hypothesis would harm the promotion of legal stability overall: for one, because the specific circumstances (allegation of harm or excessive formality in filing an appeal without meeting legal requirements) would be easily repeated or alleged by other appellants; also, not observing the legal requirements would not require any evidence that the situation was exceptional. From yet another viewpoint, that would mean that accepting the individual case would hamper the implementation of two values inherent to the rule, both supportive of one another as both relate to stability: the formal value would be restricted because the specific circumstances would be easy to repeat or allege in other appeals, forcing the court to accept thousands of irregular procedures only because of the constitutional principle of universal jurisdiction, which would generate an enormous cost given the potentially constant repetition of the situation, though such cost would not necessarily be the price for the individual decisions; and the substantive value for the parties involved would be reduced because acceptance of the behavior would have great unpredictability regarding the applicable rules and the content of the discussions. The attempt of doing justice for one case by outweighing the rule would affect the promotion of justice for the most part of the cases. And not outweighing the rule would do more good than harm.

One may quickly observe the difference between these two cases: for one, there is a case in which the individual decision, though incompatible with the general rule, does not harm the promotion of the goal underlying the rule or the legal stability of rules, since hardly will a similar situation happen or be proven again. On the other angle, there is a case in which the individual decision would restrict the promotion of the goal underlying the rule as well as the stability that sustains rules, since the specific situation has a great likelihood of happening frequently and a particular decision would create an excessive cost not necessarily justifiable by the promotion of individual justice.[158]

The study of these cases shows that a rule's degree of resistance to outweighing is related to the promotion of the value underlying the rule (specific substantive value) as well as to the realization of the formal value underlying rules (formal value of legal stability). And the degree of promotion of stability is related to the possibility of a new instance of a similar situation happening. By combining these factors, one may say that the resistance to outweighing a rule will be greater the more important legal stability is for its interpretation. Legal stability will be the more important the greater the underlying value of the stability principle for the interpretation of the matter embedded in the rule. That happens, for example, in sectors of the legal order in which the role of legal stability is prominent, such as Criminal Law and Tax Law. In these normative fields, the use of norms is important, and rigidity ought to be greater, as greater is the necessity of generalization and less harmful is the individual decision for the implementation of the general principle of equality. Secondly, legal stability will be the more important as greater is the binding of such overlying value with the value underlying the rule. That is the case when the principle of legal stability is important for the sector within which the rule is, and the goal underlying the rule is related to the promotion of stability.

Therefore, resistance to outweighing will be very small in the cases where expanding or restricting the rule hypothesis because of its goal is indifferent to legal stability. And it will be greater, as outweighing becomes more harmful to legal stability. This is so because rules determine means the Legislative uses to eliminate or reduce controversy, uncertainty and arbitrariness, on one end, and avoid problems of coordination, deliberation and discovery that exist in a custom-tailored decision model. Rules are, therefore, instruments of justice in general. The degree of resistance of the rule ought to be greater as the attempt to do justice in a particular case by outweighing a rule affects the promotion of justice for the greater part of the cases. And the degree of resistance of a rule ought to be smaller when its attempt to do justice in a particular case affects less the promotion of justice for the greater part of the cases.

The cases mentioned above also show that outweighing a rule does not require only a simple balancing of the principle of legal stability against another specific constitutional principle, as is the case of horizontal and direct balancing of constitutional principles. Defeasibility to a certain degree involves weighing such principles, but of a different kind than that of the direct balancing of colliding constitutional principles. This is so because outweighing a rule is not limited to the solution of a single case, as in the horizontal balancing of principles through the creation of concrete colliding rules; rather, it requires the construction of the solution of a case through an analysis of its impact over the greater part of cases. The individual decision to outbalance a rule must always consider its impact on the application of rules in general. Outbalancing *a rule* depends on the general applicability of *rules* and on the balance between general and individual justice the legal system intends.

2.4.9.3.2.3. Procedural requirements

The previous considerations demonstrate that rules in general (not to mention, for now, the matter concerning the existence of indefeasible conceptual rules) can be outweighed, as long as specific requirements exist. The model herein proposed not only requires the observance of some content requirements to outweigh rules, but also presents the need for some formal requirements.

As rules are immediately descriptive of conducts or assignments of power for the adoption of conducts, and it is the judge's job to apply the rule whose concept ultimately corresponds to the concept of the facts, its horizontal resistance efficacy is greater than that of principles. Indeed, rules have a decisive aspect that principles do not, as rules set forth a decision for a conflict of reasons, and judges cannot simply substitute their reasoning for that of the legislators. Rules have the ability to define principles, meaning several ideals whose realization is mandated by principles are already "ruled" on, and judges cannot realize the constitutional goal in a different manner than that set forth by the Constitution. Rules have this trench aspect since they can only be outweighed for extraordinary reasons and a great burden of justification.

This characteristic makes rules more resistant to outbalancing. And this greater resistance leads to the need of a more restrictive justification to allow outbalancing rules.

The outbalancing of a rule will require, firstly, a proper justification. Such justification depends on two factors. The first is a demonstration of the incompatibility between the rule hypothesis and its underlying goal. One ought to find the discrepancy between that which the rule sets forth and that which its goal requires. The second is the demonstration that not using the rule will not cause excessive instability to the legal system. Indeed, rules are means the Legislative uses to eliminate or reduce controversy, uncertainty, and arbitrariness, thus avoiding problems of coordination, deliberation and discovery. Therefore, rule defeasibility requires the demonstration that the general model will not be significantly affected by an excessive increase in controversy, uncertainty and arbitrariness, or by a great lack of coordination, high costs of deliberation, or serious problems in reaching discovery. In sum, outweighing a rule requires the demonstration that individual justice does not substantially affect justice in general.

Secondly, outweighing a rule ought to have a proper justification: one ought to express the reasons for outweighing in a rational and transparent manner. That is to say, a rule cannot be outweighed unless the corresponding reasons are expressed, which allows their control. The justification ought to be written, founded in legal issues and logically organized.

Thirdly, outweighing a rule ought to have proper proof: the absence of an excessive increase in controversies, uncertainty and arbitrariness, and the absence of problems of coordination, high costs of deliberation and serious problems of discovery are not obvious, neither can they be assumed. Thus arises the need for appropriate evidence, such as documents, expert opinions and statistics. Mere allegation cannot be enough to overcome a rule.

Having analyzed how legal norms cause effects, one must then analyze how they are applied. Let us then examine the normative postulates.

NOTES

1. GUASTINI, Riccardo. *Teoria e dogmatica delle fonti*. Milan: Giuffrè, 1998. p. 16. Idem. *Dalle fonti alle norme*. Turin: Giappichelli, 1992. p. 20 and on.
2. GUASTINI, Riccardo. Interprétation et description de normes. Paul Amselek, org.. *In: Interpretation et Droit*. Brussels: Bruylant, 1995. pp. 97–98.
3. MÜLLER, Friedrich. Warum Rechtslinguistik? Gemeinsame Probleme von Sprachwissenschaft und Rechtstheorie. In: ERBGUTH, Wilfried; MÜLLER, Friedrich; Neumann, Volker, org. *Rechtstheorie und Rechtsdogmatik im Austausch. Gedächtnisschrift für Bernd Jeand'Heur*. Berlin: Duncker und Humblot, 1999. p. 40. HERBERT, Manfred. *Rechtstheorie als Sprachkritik. Zum Einfluß Wittgensteins auf die Rechtstheorie*. Baden-Baden: Nomos, 1995. p. 290.
4. GRAU, Eros Roberto. *Interpretação/Aplicação do Direito*. São Paulo: Malheiros, 2002. pp. 20, 54, 69, 71, 73. CARVALHO, Paulo de Barros. *Curso de Direito Tributário*. 14th ed. São Paulo: Malheiros, 2002. p. 8.
5. GRAU, Eros Roberto. *Interpretação/Aplicação do Direito*. São Paulo: Malheiros, 2002. p. 73 and on. KAUFMANN, Arthur. *Analogie und 'Natur der Sache'*. 2nd ed. Heidelberg: Muller, 1982. p. 37 and on. Idem. Die ipsa res iusta. *In: Beiträge zur Juristischen Hermeneutik*. 2nd ed. Cologne: Carl Heymanns, 1993. p. 58.
6. WITTGENSTEIN, Ludwig. *Tratado Lógico-Filosófico – Investigações Filosóficas*. Trad. M. S. Lourenço. Lisboa: Calouste Gulbenkian, 1981. p. 263. AARNIO, Aulis. *Reason and Authority. A Treatise on the Dynamic Paradigm of Legal Dogmatics*. Aldershot: Ashgate, 1997. p. 113.
7. Cf. ZARADER, Marlene. *Heidegger et lês paroles de l'origine*. Paris: Librairie Philosophique J. VRIN, 1986. p. 54. STEIN, Ernildo. We cannot say the same in other words. ZILLES, Urbano, org. *Miguel Reale: Estudos em homenagem a seus 90 anos*. Porto Alegre: EDIPUCRS, 2000. p. 489.
8. REALE, Miguel. *Cinco temas do culturalismo*. São Paulo: Saraiva, 2000. p. 30 and 40.
9. AARNIO, Aulis. *Denkweisen der Rechtswissenschaft*. Vienna: Springer, 1979. p. 159.
10. This issue is detailed in: ÁVILA, Humberto Bergmann. Estatuto do Contribuinte: conteúdo e alcance. *Revista da Associação Brasileira de Direito Tributário* (07):73–104, Belo Horizonte: Del Rey, set/dez. 2000.
11. Concerning that matter in Brazilian Law, see especially: GRAU, Eros Roberto. *Interpretação/Aplicação do Direito*. São Paulo: Malheiros, 2002. ROTHENBURG, Walter Claudius. *Princípios constitucionais*. Porto Alegre: Fabris, 1999. If abroad, see: CANOTILHO, J. J. Gomes. *Direito Constitucional e Teoria da Constituição*. 3rd ed. Coimbra: Almedina, 1999. p. 1086 and on. FIGUEROA, Alfonso García. *Principios y positivismo jurídico*. Madrid: Centro de Estudios Políticos y Constitucionales, 1998.

12. ESSER, Josef. *Grundsatz und Norm in der richterlichen Fortbildung des Privatrechts*. 4th printing. Tübingen: Mohr Siebeck, 1990. p. 51.
13. Idem, ibidem. p. 51.
14. LARENZ, Karl. *Richtiges Recht*. Munich: Beck, 1979, p. 26. LARENZ, *Karl. Methodenlehre der Rechtswissenschaft*. 6th ed. Munich: Beck, 1991, p. 474.
15. LARENZ, Karl. *Richtiges Recht*. Munich: Beck, 1979. p. 23.
16. CANARIS, Claus-Wilhelm. *Systemdenken und Systembegriff in der Jurisprudenz*. Berlin: Duncker und Humblot, 1983, pp. 50, 53 and 55.
17. DWORKIN, Ronald. The Model of Rules, *University of Chicago Law Review* 35 (1967), p. 14 and on.
18. DWORKIN, Ronald. The Model of Rules, *University of Chicago Law Review* 35 (1967), p. 22. Idem, Is law a system of rules? *In: The Philosophy of Law,* ed. by R. M. Dworkin. Oxford: Oxford University Press, 1977. p. 43.
19. DWORKIN, Ronald. *Taking Rights Seriously*. 6th printing. London: Duckworth, 1991. p. 26. Idem, Is law a system of rules? *In: The Philosophy of Law,* ed. by R. M. Dworkin. Oxford: Oxford University Press, 1977. p. 45.
20. Idem, *Taking Rights Seriously*. 6th printing. London: Duckworth, 1991. p. 26.
21. ALEXY, Robert. Zum Begriff des Rechtsprinzips. In: Argumentation und Hermeneutik in der Jurisprudenz. *Rechtstheorie*, Beiheft 1. Berlin: Dunckler und Humblot, 1979: p. 65.
22. ALEXY, Robert. Zum Begriff des Rechtsprinzips. In: Argumentation und Hermeneutik in der Jurisprudenz. *Rechtstheorie*, Beiheft 1. Berlin: Duncker und Humblot, 1979. p. 59 and on. Idem, *Recht, Vernunft und Diskurs*. Frankfurt am Main: Suhrkamp, 1995. p. 177. Idem, Rechtsregeln und Rechtsprinzipien. *Archives Rechts und Sozialphilosophie*, Beiheft 25, 1985, p. 19 and on. Idem, Rechtssystem und praktische Vernunft. In: Recht, Vernunft, Diskurs. Frankfurt am Main: Suhrkamp, 1995. p. 216–217. Idem, *Theorie der Grundrechte*. 2nd ed. Frankfurt am Main: Suhrkamp, 1994, p. 77 and on.
23. ALEXY, Robert. Rechtsregeln und Rechtsprinzipien, *Archives Rechts und Sozialphilosophie*, Beiheft 25 (1985), p. 17.
24. Idem, ibidem, p. 18.
25. Idem, ibidem, p. 18.
26. Idem. *Theorie der Grundrechte*. 2nd ed. Frankfurt am Main: Suhrkamp, 1994. p. 80 and 83. Idem. Zum Begriff des Rechtsprinzips. In: Argumentation und Hermeneutik in der Jurisprudenz. *Rechtstheorie*, Beiheft 1. Berlin: Duncker und Humblot, 1979. p. 70.
27. Idem. Robert. Rechtsregeln und Rechtsprinzipien, *Archives Rechts und Sozialphilosophie*, Beiheft 25 (1985), p. 19. Idem. Zum Begriff des Rechtsprinzips, in: Argumentation und Hermeneutik in der Jurisprudenz, *Rechtstheorie*, Beiheft 1, Dunckler und Humblot, Berlin, (1979): 70.
28. ALEXY, Robert. Rechtsregeln und Rechtsprinzipien. *Archives Rechts und Sozialphilosophie*, Beiheft 25 (1985). p. 21.
29. ALEXY, Robert. *Rechtssystem und praktische Vernunft*. In: Recht, Vernunft, Diskurs. Frankfurt am Main: Suhrkamp, 1995. pp. 216–217; Idem. *Theorie der Grundrechte*. 2nd ed. Frankfurt am Main: Suhrkamp, 1994. p. 77.

30. ALEXY, Robert. Rechtsregeln und Rechtsprinzipien, *Archives Rechts und Sozialphilosophie*, Beiheft 25 (1985), p. 20.
31. DWORKIN, Ronald. *Takings Rights Seriously*. 6th printing. London: Duckworth, p. 24: *"If the facts a rule stipulates are given, then either the rule is valid, in which case the answer it supplies ought to be accepted, or it is not, in which case it contributes nothing to the decision"*.
32. ALEXY, Robert. Rechtssystem und praktische Vernunft. *In: Recht, Vernunft, Diskurs*. Frankfurt am Main: Suhrkamp, 1995. pp. 216–217. Idem. *Theorie der Grundrechte*. 2nd ed. Frankfurt am Main: Suhrkamp, 1994. p. 77.
33. ESSER, Josef. *Grundsatz und Norm in der richterlichen Fortbildung des Privatrechts*, 4th printing. Tübingen: Mohr Siebeck, 1990. p. 51.
34. LARENZ, Karl. *Richtiges Recht*. München: Beck, 1979, p. 26. LARENZ, *Karl. Methodenlehre der Rechtswissenschaft*. 6th ed. Munich: Beck, 1991. p. 474.
35. SOBOTA, Katharina. *Das Prinzip Rechtsstaat*. Tübingen: Mohr Siebeck, 1997. p. 415. STELZER, Manfred. *Das Wesensgehaltsargument und der Grundsatz der Verhältnismäßigkeit*. Vienna: Springer, 1991. p. 215.
36. SCHAUER, Frederick. *Playing by the rules. A philosophical Examination of Rule-Based Decision-Making in Law and in Life*. Oxford: Clarendon, 1991. p. 23; GUASTINI, Riccardo. *Distinguendo: studi dei teoria e metateoria del diritto*. Turin: Giappichelli, 1996. p. 120.
37. STELZER, Manfred. *Das Wesensgehaltsargument und der Grundsatz der Verhältnismäßigkeit*. Vienna: Springer, 1991. p. 215.
38. ECKHOFF, Torstein. Legal Principles. In: *Prescriptive Formality and Normative Rationality in Modern Legal Systems*. Festschrift for Robert S. Summers. Berlin: Duncker und Humblot, p. 38.
39. WRIGHT, Georg Henrik von. Sein und Sollen. In: *Normen, Werte und Handlungen*. Frankfurt am Main: Suhrkamp, 1994. p. 36.
40. DWORKIN, Ronald. *Taking Rights Seriously*. 6th printing. London: Duckworth, 1991. p. 26. Idem, Is law a system of rules? In: The Philosophy of Law, ed. by R. M. Dworkin. Oxford: Oxford University Press, 1977. p. 45.
41. DWORKIN, Ronald. *Takings Rights Seriously*. 6th printing. London: Duckworth, 1991. p. 24.
42. ALEXY, Robert. Rechtssystem und praktische Vernunft. *In: Recht, Vernunft, Diskurs*. Frankfurt am Main: Suhrkamp, 1995. pp. 216–217; Idem. *Theorie der Grundrechte*. 2nd ed. Frankfurt am Main: Suhrkamp, 1994. p. 77.
43. ALEXY, Robert. Rechtsregeln und Rechtsprinzipien. *In: Archives Rechts und Sozialphilosophie*, Beiheft 25 (1985), p. 20.
44. Habeas Corpus nº 73662-9, Second Bench, Opinion by Justice Marco Aurélio, D.J. Sept. 20, 1996.
45. Habeas Corpus nº 77.003-4, Second Bench, Opinion by Justice Marco Aurélio, D.J. Sept. 11, 1998.
46. Proceedings nº 13003.000021/99-14, Second Chamber of the Second Council of Taxpayers. Session held on Oct. 18, 2000.

47. GÜNTHER, Klaus. *Der Sinn für Angemessenheit. Anwendungsdiskurse in Moral und Recht*. Frankfurt am Main: Suhrkamp, 1988. p. 270.
48. ÁVILA, Humberto Bergmann. Argumentação jurídica e a imunidade dos livros eletrônicos. *Revista de Direito Tributário* (79):163–183. São Paulo: Malheiros, 2001.
49. Concerning that reservation, also ALEXY, Robert. Zum Begriff des Rechtsprinzips. *In: Argumentation und Hermeneutik in der Jurisprudenz, Rechtstheorie*, Beiheft 1, Berlin: Dunckler und Humblot, (1979): 71.
50. GUASTINI, Riccardo. *Distinguendo: studi dei teoria e metateoria del diritto*. Turin: Giappichelli, 1996. p. 120. FIGUEROA, Alfonso García. Principios y positivismo jurídico. Madrid: Centro de Estudios Políticos y Constitucionales, 1998. p. 140.
51. Concerning this matter, see: FIGUEROA, Alfonso García. *Principios y positivismo jurídico*. Madrid: Centro de Estudios Políticos y Constitucionales, 1998. p. 152.
52. SUMMERS, Robert. Two Types of Substantive Reasons: The Core of a Theory of Common-Law Justification. *The Jurisprudence of Law's Form and Substance (Collected Essays in Law)*. Aldershot: Ashgate, 2000. pp. 155–236 (224). MacCORMICK, Neil. Aargumentation and Interpretation in Law. Ratio Juris v. 6. nº 1, p. 17. London: Blackwell, 1993.
53. SCHAUER, Frederick. *Playing by the rules. A philosophical Examination of Rule-Based Decision-Making in Law and in Life*. Oxford: Clarendon, 1991. p. 38 and on.
54. DWORKIN, Ronald. *Taking Rights Seriously*. 6th printing. London: Duckworth, 1991. p. 24. ALEXY, Robert. Rechtssystem und praktische Vernunft. *In: Recht, Vernunft, Diskurs*. Frankfurt am Main: Suhrkamp, 1995. pp. 216–217. Idem. *Theorie der Grundrechte*. 2nd ed. Frankfurt am Main: Suhrkamp, 1994. p. 77.
55. HAGE, Jaap. C. *Reasoning with Rules. An Essay on Legal Reasoning and Its Underlying Logic*. Dordrecht: Kluwer, 1997. p. 5 and 118.
56. CANARIS, Claus-Wilhelm. *Systemdenken und Systembegriff in der Jurisprudenz*. Berlin: Duncker und Humblot, 1983. pp. 50, 53 and 55.
57. DWORKIN, Ronald. *Taking Rights Seriously*. 6th printing. London: Duckworth, 1991. p. 26.
58. ALEXY, Robert. Zum Begriff des Rechtsprinzips, *Rechtstheorie* Beiheft 1(1979), p. 59 and on. Idem, *Recht, Verfunft, Diskurs*. Frankfurt: Suhrkamp, 1995. p. 177. Idem, Rechtsregeln und Rechtsprinzipien. *In: Archives Rechts und Sozialphilosophie,* Beiheft 25 (1985), p. 19 e ss. Idem, Rechtssystem und praktische Vernunft. *In: Recht, Vernunft, Diskurs*. Frankfurt am Main: Suhrkamp, 1995. pp. 216–217; Idem, *Theorie der Grundrechte*. 2nd ed. Frankfurt am Main: Suhrkamp, 1994. p. 77 and on.
59. ALEXY, Robert. Rechtsregeln und Rechtsprinzipien. In: *Archives Rechts und Sozialphilosophie*, Beiheft 25 (1985), p. 17.
60. ALEXY, Robert. Rechtsregeln und Rechtsprinzipien, *Archives Rechts und Sozialphilosophie*, Beiheft 25 (1985), p. 19. Idem. Zum Begriff des Rechtsprinzips, in: Argumentation und Hermeneutik in der Jurisprudenz, *Rechtstheorie*, Beiheft 1, Dunckler und Humblot, Berlin, (1979): 70.
61. PECZENIK, Aleksander. *On law and Reason*. Dordrecht: Kluwer, 1989. p. 61.
62. Concerning the matter, see the brilliant opinion of Justice ARAKEN DE ASSIS on Agravo de Instrumento Appeal nº 598.398.600, 4th Civil Chamber, Supreme Court of

the State of Rio Grande do Sul, entered on Nov. 25, 1998. In: Jurisprudência Administrativa, Síntese Trabalhista, nº 121, July 1999, Porto Alegre: Síntese. pp. 115–119.

63. SCHAUER, Frederick. *Playing by the rules. A philosophical Examination of Rule-Based Decision-Making in Law and in Life*. Oxford: Clarendon, 1991. p. 14.
64. DWORKIN, Ronald. *Takings Rights Seriously*. 6th printing. London: Duckworth, p. 24.
65. PECZENIK, Aleksander. *On law and Reason*. Dordrecht: Kluwer, 1989. pp. 63, 80, 412 e 420. PECZENIK, Aleksander. The passion for reason. *In: The Law in Philosophical Perspectives*. Ed. Luc J. Wintgens. Dordrecht: Kluwer, 1999. p. 183.
66. SCHAUER, Frederick. *Playing by the rules. A philosophical Examination of Rule-Based Decision-Making in Law and in Life*. Oxford: Clarendon, 1991. p. 35.
67. PECZENIK, Aleksander. The passion for reason. *In: The Law in Philosophical Perspectives*. Ed. Luc J. Wintgens. Dordrecht: Kluwer, 1999. p. 181.
68. SCHAUER, Frederick. *Playing by the rules.A philosophical Examination of Rule-Based Decision-Making in Law and in Life*. Oxford: Clarendon, 1991. pp. 47 and 59.
69. SCHAUER, Frederick. *Playing by the rules. A philosophical Examination of Rule-Based Decision-Making in Law and in Life*. Oxford: Clarendon, 1991. p. 94 and on.
70. SUMMERS, Robert. Two Types of Substantive Reasons: The Core of a Theory of Common-Law Justification. *The Jurisprudence of Law's Form and Substance (Collected Essays in Law)*. Aldershot: Ashgate, 2000. pp. 155–236 (231). ALEXY, Robert. Rechtsregeln und Rechtsprinzipien, Archives Rechts und Sozialphilosophie, Beiheft 25 (1985), p. 28.
71. PECZENIK, Aleksander. The passion for reason. *In: The Law in Philosophical Perspectives*. Ed. Luc J. Wintgens. Dordrecht: Kluwer, 1999. p. 181.
72. PECZENIK, Aleksander. *On law and Reason*. Dordrecht: Kluwer, 1989. p. 80.
73. PECZENIK, Aleksander. *On law and Reason*. Dordrecht: Kluwer, 1989. p. 81.
74. GÜNTHER, Klaus. *Der Sinn für Angemessenheit. Anwendungsdiskurse in Moral und Recht*. Frankfurt am Main: Suhrkamp, 1988. p. 272. CANARIS, Claus-Wilhelm. *Die Feststellung von Lücken im Gesetz*. Berlin: Duncker und Humblot, 1982.
75. HAGE, Jaap. C. *Reasoning with Rules. An Essay on Legal Reasoning and Its Underlying Logic*. Dordrecht: Kluwer, 1997. p. 116.
76. Recurso Extraordinário Appeal nº 216.541-7, First Bench, Opinion by Justice Sepúlveda Pertence, DJ May 5, 1998.
77. Agravo Regimental em Agravo de Petição nº 282522, First Bench, Opinion by Justice Moreira Alves, DJ Aug. 31, 2001.
78. HAGE, Jaap. C. *Reasoning with Rules. An Essay on Legal Reasoning and Its Underlying Logic*. Dordrecht: Kluwer, 1997. pp. 34 e 116.
79. GÜNTHER, Klaus. *Der Sinn für Angemessenheit. Anwendungsdiskurse in Moral und Recht*. Frankfurt am Main: Suhrkamp, 1988. p. 273.
80. ALEXY, Robert. Rechtsregeln und Rechtsprinzipien. *Archives Rechts und Sozialphilosophie*, Beiheft 25 (1985), p. 19: "möglichst hohen Masse realisiert wird".
81. PENSKY, Ulrich. Rechtsgrunsätze und Rechtsregeln. In: *Juristen Zeitung*, 3 (1989) 109.

82. PENSKY, Ulrich. Rechtsgrunsätze und Rechtsregeln. In: *Juristen Zeitung*, 3 (1989): 109.
83. Idem, ibidem, p. 110.
84. AARNIO, *Aulis. Reason and Authority*. Aldershot: Ashgate, 1997. p. 181.
85. ALEXY, Robert. My Philosophy of Law: The Institutionalisation of Reason. *In: The Law in Philosophical Perspectives*. Ed. Luc Wintgens. Dordrecht: Kluwer, 1999. p. 39. Idem. On the structure of legal principles. *Ratio Juris* (13):300, Oxford: Blackwell, 2000.
86. WRIGHT, Georg Henrik von. Sein und Sollen. In: *Normen, Werte und Handlungen*. Frankfurt am Main: Suhrkamp, 1994. p. 36.
87. AARNIO, Aulis. *Denkweisen der Rechtswissenschaft*. Vienna: Springer, 1979. p. 158.
88. Concerning the "discharge function" (*Entlastungsfunktion*) of dogmatics, see: ALEXY, Robert. *Theorie der juristischen Argumentation*. 2nd ed. Frankfurt: Suhrkamp, 1991. p. 329.
89. JESTAEDT, Matthias. *Grundrechtsentfaltung im Gesetz*. Tübingen: Siebeck, 1999. p. 231.
90. PECZENIK, Aleksander. *On law and Reason*. Dordrecht: Kluwer, 1989. p. 82.
91. About the meaning of heuristic value: SCHEPERS, H. Heuristik. *In: Historisches Wörterbuch der Philosophie*. Darmstadt: Wissenschaftliche Buchgesellschaft, 1974. v. 3. p. 1119. HAGE, Jaap. C. *Reasoning with Rules. An Essay on Legal Reasoning and Its Underlying Logic*. Dordrecht: Kluwer, 1997. p. 121. FERRAZ Jr. Tércio. *Função social da dogmática jurídica*. São Paulo: Max Limonad, 1997. p. 123.
92. MICHAEL, Lothar. *Der allgemeine Gleichheitssatz als Methodennorm komparativer Systeme*. Berlin: Duncker und Humblot, 1997. p. 48.
93. GRECO, Marco Aurélio. *Contribuições (uma figura "sui generis")*. São Paulo: Dialética, 2000. p. 168.
94. MENDONÇA, Maria Luiza Vianna Pessoa de. *O princípio constitucional da irretroatividade da lei*. Belo Horizonte: Del Rey, 1996. p. 59 and on.
95. DERZI, Misabel de Abreu Machado. Notas a BALEEIRO, Aliomar. *Limitações constitucionais ao Poder de Tributar*. 7. ed. Rio de Janeiro: Forense, 1997. p. 228.
96. PESTANA, Márcio. *O princípio da imunidade tributária*. São Paulo: Revista dos Tribunais, 2001. p. 63.
97. LESSA, Pedro. *In: Biblioteca Internacional de Obras Célebres*. Volume XI. Lisbon: Sociedade Internacional, [19–]. p. 1049.
98. About the issue, see: FIGUEROA, Alfonso García. *Principios y positivismo jurídico*. Madrid: Centro de Estudios Políticos y Constitucionales, 1998. p. 151.
99. ÁVILA, Humberto Bergmann. A distinção entre princípios e regras e a redefinição do dever de proporcionalidade. *RDA* (215):151–152, Rio de Janeiro: Renovar, jan./mar. 1999.
100. WRIGHT, Georg von. *Rationalität: Mittel und Zwecke*. In: *Normen, Werte und Handlungen*. Frankfurt am Main: Suhrkamp, 1994. p. 127.
101. HAGE, Jaap. C. *Reasoning with Rules. An Essay on Legal Reasoning and Its Underlying Logic*. Dordrecht: Kluwer, 1997. p. 67.

102. AARNIO, Aulis. *Reason and Authority. A Treatise on the Dynamic Paradigm of Legal Dogmatics*. Aldershot: Ashgate, 1997. p. 183. PECZENIK, Aleksander. On law and Reason. Dordrecht: Kluwer, 1989. p. 74.
103. WRIGHT, Georg Henrik von. Sein und Sollen. In: *Normen, Werte und Handlungen*. Frankfurt am Main: Suhrkamp, 1994. p. 36.
104. HAGE, Jaap. C. *Reasoning with Rules. An Essay on Legal Reasoning and Its Underlying Logic*. Dordrecht: Kluwer, 1997. p. 67.
105. AARNIO, Aulis. *Reason and Authority. A Treatise on the Dynamic Paradigm of Legal Dogmatics*. Aldershot: Ashgate, 1997. p. 181.
106. See, about the different kinds of goal norms: SOMMERMANN, Karl-Peter. *Staatsziele und Staatszielbestimmungen*. Tübingen: Mohr Siebeck, 1997. p. 355 and on.
107. SUMMERS, Robert. Two Types of Substantive Reasons: The Core of a Theory of Common-Law Justification. *The Jurisprudence of Law's Form and Substance (Collected Essays in Law)*. Aldershot: Ashgate, 2000. pp. 155–236 (224).
108. HAGE, Jaap. C. *Reasoning with Rules. An Essay on Legal Reasoning and Its Underlying Logic*. Dordrecht: Kluwer, 1997. p. 116.
109. CANARIS, Claus-Wilhelm. Theorienrezeption und Theorienstruktur. *In: Wege zum japanischen Recht. Festschrift für Zentaro Kitagawa*. Hans G. Leser, org. Berlin: Duncker und Humblot, 1992. pp. 59–94.
110. SUMMERS, Robert. Two Types of Substantive Reasons: The Core of a Theory of Common-Law Justification. *The Jurisprudence of Law's Form and Substance (Collected Essays in Law)*. Aldershot: Ashgate, 2000. pp. 155–236 (224).
111. SUMMERS, Robert. Two Types of Substantive Reasons: The Core of a Theory of Common-Law Justification. *The Jurisprudence of Law's Form and Substance (Collected Essays in Law)*. Aldershot: Ashgate, 2000. pp. 155–236 (169).
112. HAGE, Jaap. C. *Reasoning with Rules. An Essay on Legal Reasoning and Its Underlying Logic*. Dordrecht: Kluwer, 1997. p. 116.
113. WEINBERGER, Ota. *Rechtslogik*. 2nd ed. Berlin: Duncker und Humblot, 1989. p. 283.
114. MODESTO, Paulo. Controle jurídico do comportamento ético da administração pública no Brasil. *RDA* (209):77, Rio de Janeiro: Renovar, 1997.
115. WEINBERGER, Ota. *Rechtslogik*. 2nd ed. Berlin: Duncker und Humblot, 1989. p. 287.
116. ALEXY, Robert. Rechtsregeln und Rechtsprinzipien, *Archives Rechts und Sozialphilosophie*, Beiheft 25 (1985), p. 24. GRAU, Eros Roberto. *Interpretação/Aplicação do Direito*. São Paulo: Malheiros, 2002. p. 42.
117. CANARIS, Claus-Wilhelm. Theorienrezeption und Theorienstruktur. *In: Wege zum japanischen Recht. Festschrift für Zentaro Kitagawa*. Org. Hans G. Leser. Berlin: Duncker und Humblot, 1992. pp. 59–94.
118. GUASTINI, Riccardo. *Il giudice e la legge*. Turin: Giappichelli, 1995. pp. 136 and on. AARNIO, Aulis. *Reason and Authority*. Dartmouth: Ashgate, 1997. pp. 160 and on.
119. AARNIO, Aulis. *Reason and Authority: A Treatise on the Dynamic Paradigm of Legal Dogmatics*. Aldershot: Ashgate, 1997. p. 174.
120. ÁVILA, Humberto. *Sistema Constitucional Tributário*. São Paulo: Saraiva, 2004. p. 153.
121. ÁVILA, Humberto. *Sistema Constitucional Tributário*. São Paulo: Saraiva, 2004. p. 53.

122. CANARIS, Claus-Wilhelm. Funktion, Struktur und Falsifikation juristischer Theorien. *Juristen Zeitung* Nr. 8, p. 377–391, 1993.
123. Recurso Extraordinário Appeal nº 192568-0, 2nd Bench, Opinion by Justice Marco Aurélio, DJ Sept 13, 1996.
124. ÁVILA, Humberto. Benefícios fiscais inválidos e a legítima expectativa dos contribuintes. *Revista Tributária* (42):100–114, São Paulo: Revista dos Tribunais, 2002.
125. Concerning the use of the term "efficacy function", read: FERRAZ Jr., Tércio Sampaio. *Introdução ao Estudo do Direito (Introduction to Jurisprudence).* 3rd ed. São Paulo: Atlas, 2001. p. 196. Concerning the use of the term "function" regarding principles read: "REALE, Miguel. *Lições preliminares de Direito (First lessons on Law).* 23rd ed. São Paulo: Saraiva, 1996. p. 300.
126. IVAINER, Thédore *L'Interprétation des faits en droit.* Paris: LGDJ, 1988. pp. 188 and on.
127. KAUFMANN, Arthur. *Analogie und Natur der Sache. Zugleich ein Beitrag zur Lehre vom Typus.* 2. ed. Heidelberg: Müller, 1982. pp. 37 and on.
128. HABERMAS, Jürgen. Wahrheitstheorien. *In: Vorstudien und Ergänzungen zur Theorie des kommunikativen Handels.* Frankfurt am Main: Suhrkamp, 1995. p. 135.
129. VARGA, Csaba. The Non-cognitive Character of the Judicial Establishment of Facts. *In: Praktische Vernunft und Rechtsanwendung. Archiv für Recht- und Sozialphilosophie,* v. 53, p. 232. Stuttgart: Franz Steiner, 1994. IVAINER, Thédore. *L'Interprétation des faits en droit.* Paris: LGDJ, 1988. p. 119.
130. VARGA, Csaba. The Non-cognitive Character of the Judicial Establishment of Facts. *In: Praktische Vernunft und Rechtsanwendung. Archiv für Recht- und Sozialphilosophie,* v. 53, p. 235. Stuttgart: Franz Steiner, 1994. CARVALHO, Paulo de Barros. *Direito Tributário: Fundamentos Jurídicos da Incidência.* São Paulo: Saraiva, 1998. p. 10.
131. IVAINER, Thédore. *L'Interprétation des faits en droit.* Paris: LGDJ, 1988. p. 135.
132. VARGA, Csaba. The Non-cognitive Character of the Judicial Establishment of Facts. *In: Praktische Vernunft und Rechtsanwendung. Archiv für Recht- und Sozialphilosophie,* v. 53, p. 232. Stuttgart: Franz Steiner, 1994.
133. ALEXANDER, Larry and SHERWIN, Emily. *The Rules of Rules – Morality, Rules and the Dilemmas of Law.* Durham and London: Duke University Press, 2001. p. 103.
134. ALEXANDER, Larry and SHERWIN, Emily. *The Rules of Rules – Morality, Rules and the Dilemmas of Law.* Durham and London: Duke University Press, 2001. p. 103.
135. BANDEIRA DE MELLO, Celso Antônio. *Curso de Direito Administrativo.* 12th ed. 2nd printing. São Paulo: Malheiros, 2000. p. 748. About this definition, read excellent article: BARCELLOS, Ana Paula. Some normative parameters for constitutional weighing. *In: A nova interpretação constitucional.* Org. Luis Roberto Barroso. Rio de Janeiro: Renovar, 2003. pp. 49 and on.
136. ALEXY, Robert. *Theorie der Grundrechte.* 2nd ed. Frankfurt am Main: Suhrkamp, 1994. p. 89.
137. Habeas Corpus nº 79.512-9, Full Court, Reported by Justice Sepúlveda Pertence, DJ 16-May-03.
138. Recurso Extraordinário Appeal nº 357950, Full Court, reported by Justice Marco Aurélio, DJ Oct. 15, 2006.

139. AARNIO, Aulis. *Reason and Authority. A Treatise on the Dynamic Paradigm of Legal Dogmatics*. Aldershot: Anshgate, 1997. p. 160 and on. BELTRÁN, Jordi Ferrer. *Las normas de competência*. Madrid: Boletín Oficial del Estado, 2000. p. 127.
140. ALEXANDER, Larry and SHERWIN, Emily. *The Rules of Rules – Morality, Rules and the Dilemmas of Law*. Durham and London: Duke University Press, 2001. p. 4.
141. GOTTLIEB, Stephen E.. The Paradox of Balancing Significant Interests. *Hastings Law Journal*. v. 45, n. 4, April 1994, p. 843.
142. ALEXANDER, Larry and SHERWIN, Emily. *The Rules of Rules – Morality, Rules and the Dilemmas of Law*. Durham and London: Duke University Press, 2001. p. 30.
143. RAZ, Joseph. *The Authority of Law – Essays on Law and Morality*. Oxford: Clarendon Press, 2002. p. 17.
144. RAZ, Joseph. *The Authority of Law – Essays on Law and Morality*. Oxford: Clarendon Press, 2002. pp. 22–23.
145. SCHAUER, Frederick. Formalism. *The Yale Law Journal*. v. 97, n. 4, March 1988, p. 537.
146. PILDES, Richard H.. Avoiding Balancing: The Role of Exclusionary Reasons in Constitutional Law. *Hastings Law Journal*. v. 45, n. 4, April 1994, p. 750.
147. PILDES, Richard H.. Avoiding Balancing: The Role of Exclusionary Reasons in Constitutional Law. *Hastings Law Journal*. v. 45, n. 4, April 1994, p. 714.
148. PILDES, Richard H.. Avoiding Balancing: The Role of Exclusionary Reasons in Constitutional Law. *Hastings Law Journal*. v. 45, n. 4, April 1994, pp. 724–725.
149. PILDES, Richard H.. Avoiding Balancing: The Role of Exclusionary Reasons in Constitutional Law. *Hastings Law Journal*. v. 45, n. 4, April 1994, p. 715.
150. SCHAUER, Frederick. Easy Cases. *Modern Constitucional Theory: a Reader*. 5th ed. Org. John Garvey, Alexander Aleinikoff and Daniel Farber. São Paulo: West, 2004. p. 130.
151. MONTAIGNE, Michel. Essais. Book III. chapter XIII. In Ouvres complètes. Paris: Éditions Gallimard, 1962.
152. ALEXANDER, Larry and SHERWIN, Emily. *The Rules of Rules – Morality, Rules and the Dilemmas of Law*. Durham and London: Duke University Press, 2001. pp. 30–31.
153. SCHAUER, Frederick. Formalism. *The Yale Law Journal*. v. 97, n. 4, March 1988, p. 543.
154. SHEPPARD, Steve. The State Interest in the Good Citizen: Constitutional Balance Between the Citizen and the Perfectionist State. *Hastings Law Journal*. v. 45, n. 4, April 1994, p. 971.
155. SCHAUER, Frederick. *Profiles, Probabilities and Stereotypes*. Cambridge: Harvard University Press, 2003. p. 53.
156. ALEXANDER, Larry and SHERWIN, Emily. *The Rules of Rules – Morality, Rules and the Dilemmas of Law*. Durham and London: Duke University Press, 2001. pp. 30–31.
157. See, about the different models of argumentation in Law: SCHAUER, Frederick. Rules and The Rule of Law. *Harvard Journal of Law and Public Policy*. V. 14, nº 3, 1991, pp. 645–694.
158. SCHAUER, Frederick. *Profiles, Probabilities and Stereotypes*. Cambridge: Harvard University Press, 2003. p. 53.

CHAPTER 3

METANORMS

Normative Postulates

3.1. INTRODUCTION

The interpretation of any cultural object is subject to some essential conditions, without which one cannot even grasp the object. Such essential conditions are called postulates.[1] There are merely hermeneutical postulates, aiming to a general understanding of the Law, and applied postulates, which aim to structure is actual application.

Applied normative postulates are direct methodological norms that present the criteria for the application of other norms on the same level as the object of the application. Therefore, they are defined as norms about the application of other norms, i.e. as metanorms. Hence they are said to be second degree norms. In that sense, whenever a normative postulate is presented, there is a methodological guideline for the interpreter concerning the interpretation of other norms. Behind postulates, there are always other norms being applied. They are not the same, however, as other norms that influence norms, such as the superprinciples of the Rule of Law and legal stability. Superprinciples are on the level of the norms which are object of the application. They act on others, but on a semantic and axiological scope and not on methodic scope, as postulates. That explains the difference between supernorms (semantically and axiologically overlying norms, located on the level of the object of the application) and metanorms (methodologically overlying norms, located on the application metalevel).

Postulates work differently from principles and rules. Firstly, because they are not on the same level: principles and rules are objects of application; postulates are norms that guide the application of others. Secondly, because the addresses are different: principles and rules are mainly directed to the Public Power and to the taxpayers; postulates are directly oriented towards those who interpret and apply the Law. Thirdly, because they relate differently with other norms: principles and rules, even because they are located on the same level as the object, influence each other, either in a preliminarily complementary way (principles) or in a decisively complementary way (rules); postulates, precisely because they are on a metalevel, guide the application of principles and rules without of necessity conflicting with other norms.

Postulates cannot be seen either as rules or as principles according to the traditional model. If rules are defined as norms that describe a behavior to be observed (or reserve a portion of power, or set forth procedures, or establish definitions, and are always followed by means of behaviors), and ought to be followed completely, and may be excluded from the legal order in case of conflict with a contrary rule, then postulates are not rules: they do not describe a behavior (nor do they reserve a portion of power, set forth procedures, or establish definitions), they are not followed completely, let alone can they be excluded from the legal order. Instead, postulates set forth methodological guidelines, which in every and by every way require a more complex application than an initial or final operation of coupling fact and norm. If principles were defined as norms that establish an ideal ought-to-be, and that can be followed in several degrees and may have a dimension of greater or smaller weight in case of conflict, then postulates are not principles: they do not set forth an ideal ought-to-be, neither are they followed in degrees, let alone is their weight variable and workable by circumstances. Instead, postulates set forth methodological guidelines, with structuring application, constant relatively to other variables.

Regardless of the preferred denomination, postulates work differently from other norms of the legal order. This reason alone is enough to study them separately. Their function and content will be better expounded. Although the denomination is secondary, the scientific requirement of syntactic compatibility does not endorse its denomination as a principle if the author defines a principle as a norm oriented to immediate goals, a norm of optimization to be realized in several degrees and according to the fact and norm possibilities, or as a norm with a high degree of abstraction and generalization. In such cases, the problem is not naming, the problem is the lack of scientific consistency. Especially since postulates are methodic, not goal-oriented; not to be realized in several degrees, but aimed at structuring the application of other norms with rigid rationality; and they are not norms with a high degree of abstraction and generalization, but norms that offer quite precise criteria for the application of the Law.

3.2. HERMENEUTIC POSTULATES

3.2.1. Overview

In Law, there are hermeneutic postulates, whose use is required to an internal and abstract understanding of the legal order, and which may support different alternatives of normative application. One of the most important is the postulate of unity of the legal order, which requires the interpreter to relate part and whole by employing order and unity categories.[2] A sub-element of this postulate is the postulate of coherence, which burdens the interpreter with many duties, one of them being the duty of relating norms to the norms that are formally or substantively superior to them.

The conditions for discovery that hermeneutics reveals are true postulates: where there is a part there is a whole; where there is an object to be discovered there is a subject to discover it; where there is a system, there is a problem.[3]

The understanding of the order as a scaled structure of norms is based on the postulate of hierarchy, from which some important criteria derive for the interpretation of norms, such as that of the interpretation according to the Constitution.

3.2.2. Postulate of Coherence

3.2.2.1. From hierarchy to coherence The issue of hierarchization of norms covers two planes that ought to be separated: a concrete plane and an abstract plane.

On a concrete plane, it matters to know which norm ought to prevail in the case of a conflict, which presupposes a concrete opposition between legal norms.

On an abstract plane, there are two problems to tackle. On one side, it matters to know whether some legal norms have a superior hierarchy, in the sense of an intrinsic preference to the legal system, either final or conditional, relative to other norms. On the other hand – and this is a completely different matter – one ought to know which dependent relations (*Abhängigkeitsbeziehungen*) exist between the legal norms of a specific legal system.

Whereas one investigates a relation of concrete prevalence and a real conflict between legal norms on the concrete plane, the abstract plane has two different aspects: a relation of abstract prevalence between norms and a connection of meaning between norms. The first case, of abstract prevalence, is usually presented as a hierarchy relation and it presupposes discovery of which norm "is worth more" or "outranks" the other. The second case, of a meaning connection, is often presented as a hierarchy relation, but it is also called internal order (*innere Einordnung*), combination of norms (*Normenkombination*) and justification connection (*Begründungszusammenhang*).

What matters is that, on a concrete plane, the relationship between norms depends on a concrete rule of preference between conflicting reasons. On an abstract plane, one may construe an argumentative structure, even without a given problem.

The question about whether there is prevalence or abstract hierarchy between legal norms, in the sense of an inherent preference order, is highly disputed.[4] A final, definitive relation of prevalence between constitutional legal norms – as will be shown – cannot be supported.[5]

What is key to this work, however, is to record that a hierarchy relation is usually associated with the idea of prevalence and ultimately points to which norm "is worth more." The notion of hierarchy involves a linear relation between two semantically separated norms, in a manner that one of them outranks the other. And, in the case of conflict, the inferior norm that is incompatible with the superior norm will lose, *ipso facto*, its validity by means of an exclusion reasoning. This systematization is classified as linear (the superior norm is the basis of the inferior norm), simple (based on a relation of linear hierarchy between norms) and non-gradable between two legal norms (norms are, or are not, systematized while in a hierarchy), with consequences on its validity.

Hierarchization can be explained in many ways. From a semiotics viewpoint, one describes a syntactic and a semantic hierarchy. The syntactic hierarchy concerns the logical relation between norms. The semantic hierarchy can be divided into two groups: formal hierarchy and substantive hierarchy. Substantive semantic hierarchy concerns formal preconditions that a norm establishes for the enactment of another. Material semantic hierarchy focuses on the preconditions of content that a norm establishes for the enactment of another.[6] The limitations that arise from these relationships can be defined as substantive limitations.[7]

From a similar perspective, encompassing not only legal norms, but also normative powers and sources, one may use the categories of formal/structural, substantive, logical, and axiological hierarchy.[8] Structural or formal hierarchy concerns the relationship between two legal norms, enacted by two branches of government, in a manner such that one derives its validity justification from the other (for example, the relation between the constitutional amending power and the constitutional power of the original framers). Substantive hierarchy concerns the relation between two legal norms, in the case of a third norm establishing that one of the two does not have a validity justification when it conflicts with another (for example, the relationship between the Constitution and Congress Acts). The logical hierarchy concerns the relationship between norms that depend on the structure of the language (for example, between an act that revokes a law and the revoked law). And the axiological hierarchy points to a relationship between norms that is not expressly regulated by Law but arises from an interpreter's assessment, which then points to the higher value of one of them.

This notion of hierarchy, though important to explain, among other phenomena, the legal order as a scaled structure of norms, is not enough to cover the complexity of relationships between legal norms. Indeed, many questions are not answered by this model. What are the relationships between rules and constitutional principles? Is it only principles that act on rules, or do rule perhaps simultaneously act on the normative content of principles? What are the relationships among the constitutional principles themselves? Do all principles have the same function, or are there any that may predetermine content at some time, and structure the application of others at other times? What are the relationships between legal rules, already sustained as valid, and the jurisdiction rules and principles the Constitution sets forth? Is it only constitutional norms that act on infraconstitutional norms, or do the latter perhaps act on the former as well?

In order to answer these questions, this work proposes a complementation to this model of linear, simple, non-gradable systematization, whose non-implementation has consequences on the validity plane. The complementation is a systematization model that is circular (superior norms condition inferior norms, and the latter contribute to determine the elements of the former), complex (not only a vertical relationship of hierarchy, but several horizontal, vertical and intertwined relationships between norms), and gradable (systematization will be more perfect the more its criteria are observed), whose main consequence is found in the plane of efficacy. Enters the postulate of coherence.

The connection of meaning or the relationship of dependence between norms is a known hermeneutical postulate: it is a condition of possibility of discovery to be met of necessity in the interpretation of normative texts.[9] Coherence is as much a criterion of the relationship between two elements as it is a property resulting from that same relationship. As BRACKER shows, a relationship is coherent when it meets formal and substantive requirements. Hence the reference to formal and substantive coherence. Formal coherence is linked to the notion on consistency and completeness. Substantive coherence is related to the positive connection of meaning.[10]

On the formal plane, a set of propositions is considered coherent if it meets the requirements of (a) consistency and (b) completeness. Consistency means lack of contradiction: a set of propositions is consistent if it does not simultaneously have a proposition and its negation. Completeness means the relationship of each element with the rest of the system, in terms of integrity (the set of propositions has all elements and their negations) and inferential cohesion (the set of propositions has its own logical consequences).

On a substantive plane, a set of propositions is considered coherent (a) the more each proposition depends on the others, and (b) the more common elements are there. Substantive coherence as a result of reciprocal dependence exists when the relationship between the propositions meets requirements of logical implication (the truth of the premise leads to the truth of the conclusion) and logical equivalence (the content of truth in one proposition acts on the content of truth of another and vice-versa). Substantive coherence as a result of common elements exists when the propositions have similar meanings. Unlike formal coherence, which either exists or not, substantive coherence can be graded. In other words: it can be greater or smaller.[11]

The use of the postulate of coherence as a complementation to that of hierarchy (taken as the static relationship between two normative sources, one at the top and another at the bottom) is important for two main reasons.

Firstly, for a better understanding of the relationship between norms. The vertical relationship between norms (e.g. constitutional and infraconstitutional norms) ought to be presented in such a manner that the meaning of the inferior norm ought to be that which "more intensely" corresponds to the meaning of the superior norm.[12] The horizontal relationship between norms (more general and more specific constitutional principles, or constitutional principles and constitutional rules, for example) ought to be understood in such a manner that the normative content of the more specific norm is precisely a "better specification" of the more general norm. In both scenarios, though, it must be clear that superior and inferior norms, and more general and more specific norms, act simultaneously one on the other: the content of the inferior norm ought to correspond to the content of the superior norm, in the same manner and at the same time that the content of the superior norm ought to be revealed by the content of the inferior norm; and the content of the more specific norm ought to correspond to the content of the more general norm, in the same manner and at the same time that the content of the more general norms ought to be revealed by the content of the more specific norms. Efficacy is reciprocal, not unidirectional.

Secondly, the postulate of coherence helps better understand the degrees of the relationships between norms. The use of the hierarchical criterion usually leads to an exclusive alternative: the inferior norm is "compatible or incompatible" with the superior norm. The use of the coherence criterion complements the notion of hierarchy to demonstrate that the relationship between norms, concerning their substantive aspect, can be graded, i.e. "more or less."[13] Some examples will show it.

In the case of concentrated control of constitutionality, the Brazilian Supreme Court and the German Constitutional Court have analyzed administrative or normative acts passed in disagreement with the Constitution. However, the Courts have issued several decisions in which they keep the effects of such acts because keeping them promotes the constitutional order "more" than not keeping them. Thus states GUSY: "*Keeping unconstitutional laws until new legislative regulation [is passed] is not only necessary, but also a constitutional obligation: they are 'closer to the Constitution' (näher am Grundgeset).*"[14]

In the case of the interpretation of constitutional rules, the Brazilian Supreme Court has chosen, among the existing interpretation alternatives, that which is "more supported" by the fundamental constitutional principles.

And, in applying the postulate of reasonableness, the Brazilian Supreme Court and the German Constitutional Court have often not applied a rule because the superior substantive principles that determine the non-application of a rule (human dignity and liberty, for example) are "more important" than the formal principles that determine the unconditional obedience to the rule (legal stability and certainty of the Law, for example).

In every case, it is no longer a choice between "promoting or not promoting," "supporting or not supporting," or "compatible or incompatible." Instead, it is a choice between "promoting more or promoting less," "supporting more or supporting less," and "more compatible or less compatible."

3.2.2.2. Substantive coherence

3.2.2.2.1. Justification by support

Firstly, justification will be the more coherent the better it is supported by another statement. That will naturally depend on the extension and intensity of the justification.[15] Extension is ensured by the search to justify the more specific statements with the more general statements. Intensity is ensured by choosing plausible premises and conclusion that are logically derived from them. The meaning connection is based on the idea of unity and coherence in the legal system, and it advises conceptual clarity, formal unity and systematic fullness.[16] The ordination of legal norms derives from the principle of equality, the generalizing tendency to justice, and legal stability, and it determines that norms ought to be oriented back to a few agglutinating principles.[17]

What is important is that this postulate has a narrow connection with the efficacy of legal norms in itself. Concrete efficacy of a constitutional norm is greater, the better, the more objectively its explanation is structured. Its efficacy depends on the capacity to justify future decisions (*Begründungsoptimierungstauglichkeit*). And the justifying capacity of a constitutional norm (more open) is better, the more intense is the relationship that it has with other constitutional norms, so as to narrow its semantic openness. The attempt for efficacy of a norm implies its substantive systematization.

Subprinciples and rules are better justified, the more intensely they are supported by superior principles.[18] Based on epistemological categories CARNAP developed to confirm and sustain statements[19], one may reach the main question dealt with herein: the direct or indirect "retroorientation" (*Zurückführbarkeit*) of a norm to a superior principle, which has a fundamental meaning in a given legal system, causes all norms derived by means of a syntactic or semantic bind to incorporate the same legal meaning of the superior norm. The relationship of dependence of a norm on a fundamental principle causes such norm, relative to other norms, to acquire the normative meaning of its justifying basis.

Concerning the limitations to the power to tax, this search for coherence is performed by concatenating several limitations, notably by agglutination of the more specific to the more general ones. That explains the classification of limitations in formal and substantive, and also justifies the binding of each subspecies to the fundamental constitutional principles. Thus, for instance, the rule of statutory legality is bound to the democratic principle and the principle of legal stability, and the rules of tax exemption are bound to the constitutional principles that present them. Even after that, one still seeks to choose, from the several plausible meanings of the norm under analysis, that which is logically and axiologically bound to the agglutinating principles.[20]

From that starting point, one may state that the construction of substantive coherence of a system ought to be done from a degree of abstraction bound to the axiological overlapping of legal norms, in the sense that the principles that have a higher degree of abstraction determine the normative meaning of the other, less abstract norms.[21]

This content justification arises when a norm with a narrower material scope of incidence relates to a norm with a more general material scope of incidence.[22] A norm has justifying meaning for another when it is more general, so that the other norms may be qualified as an "expression," "specification" or application of the former, or when it establishes a goal that encompasses other norms, so that the latter may be qualified as the "realization" of the former.[23] This construction, based on "subordinating values" is at times explained as axiological hierarchy.[24]

3.2.2.2.2. Reciprocal justification

Secondly, justification will be more coherent the more its elements justify one another. Reciprocal justification exists in a system where two elements relate in such manner that the first element belongs to a premise from which the second element logically derives, while the second element is part of a premise from which the first element also derives logically. There are three main form of reciprocal justification: empirical, analytical, and normative.

Reciprocal justification is empirical when the existence of the first element is a factual condition for the existence of the second element, and vice-versa. Thus, for example, the lasting institutionalization of fundamental rights is a factual condition for the lasting institutionalization of democracy, and vice-versa.[25] "One" is not without the factual existence of the "other," and the "other" is not without the factual existence of "one."

Reciprocal justification is analytical when the existence of the first element is a conceptual condition for the existence of the second element, and vice-versa. Thus, for example, the efficacy of fundamental rights is a necessary conceptual condition of the existence of a minimally developed Rule of Law, and the existence of a minimally developed Rule of Law is a conceptual condition of the efficacy of fundamental rights. Analytical reciprocal justification is of great value in the case of limitations to the power of taxation. Indeed, several concepts are interrelated: the federation principle conceptually presupposes financial autonomy through tax exemption, and financial autonomy through tax exemption is an element of the federation principle itself; the existence of the principle of separation of power, the democratic principle and the efficacy of fundamental rights are necessary conceptual conditions for the existence of the principle of the Rule of Law, and the existence of the principle of the Rule of Law is a necessary conceptual condition for the existence of each of those elements..

Reciprocal justification is normative when two different arguments may be combined together: the justification of more than one specific statement by a more general statement (deductive justification) and the justification of a more general statement by a more specific statement (inductive justification).[26] Likewise, normative reciprocal justification is of great importance in the case of the limitations to the power to tax. For instance, the rules of statutory legality, non-retroactivity, and previous enactment are elements that combine together in an ascending course of meaning to produce the principle of legal stability, which acts on the interpretation of the meaning of the rules of statutory legality, non-retroactivity, and previous enactment. As can be seen, systematization is circular and not simply linear.

3.3. APPLICATIVE POSTULATES

The concrete understanding of the Law requires the implementation of some conditions. These conditions are defined as applied normative postulates, as they are applied to solve questions that arise from the application of the Law, mostly to solve occasional, concrete, and external antinomies: occasional, not mandatory, because they arise from time to time depending on each case; concrete, not abstract, because the arise from an actual problem; and external, not internal, because they do not arise from conflicts within the legal order, but from circumstances foreign to it.[27] Some of the main applied postulates are those of proportionality, reasonableness, and prohibition of excess, which will be analyzed in detail further on.

This work has so far attempted to investigate principles that, as such, set forth purposes to be achieved. From now on, the duty of promoting a state of affairs will no longer be examined. Instead, the focus will be on how this duty ought to be applied. The scope of norms has been overcome as we now enter the field of metanorms. These duties are at a second level and set forth the application structure of other norms, principles and rules. As such, they allow identifying cases where there are violations to the norms whose application they support. Only elliptically can one say that the postulates of reasonableness, proportionality or efficiency, for instance, are violated. Actually, it is the norms – principles and rules – not duly applied that are violated.

For instance, in the case the Supreme Court ruled as unconstitutional a state statute that provided for weighing gas bottles in from of consumers, the principle of free initiative was considered violated because it was restrained unnecessarily and disproportionately.[28] Actually, it was not *proportionality* that was violated, but free initiative on its horizontal interrelation with the principle of consumer protection, which was not appropriately applied. Likewise, in the case the Supreme Court reversed the legal order to compel a patient to take a DNA test, the patient's human dignity was considered violated as having been unnecessarily and disproportionately restricted.[29] Strictly speaking, it was not *proportionality* that was violated, but the principle of human dignity on its horizontal interrelation with the principles of self-determination of personality and universal jurisdiction, which were not appropriately applied. The same applies to reasonableness as will be shown later on.

These considerations lead to an understanding that normative postulates are at a different level from that of the norms whose application they scaffold. Violating them consists of not interpreting them according to their scaffolding. Therefore, they are metanorms or second level norms. Their classification as second level norms, though, ought not to lead to the conclusion that normative postulates operate as any norm that justifies the application of other norms, as is the case with superprinciples such as the Rule of Law or the due process of law. That is so because these superprinciples are located at the same level as the norms that are subject to application, and not at the level of the norms that scaffold the application of others. Also, superprinciples operate as formal and substantive foundation for defining and assigning meaning to hierarchically inferior norms, whereas normative postulates scaffold the application of other norms.

The definition of normative applicative postulates as scaffolding duties of the application of other norms introduces the question of whether they can be considered as principles or rules. ALEXY does not directly classify proportionality under a specific category, using the term "principle" (*Grundsatz*) to define it and stating in a footnote that partial maxims can be classified as rules.[30] The most part of jurisprudence classifies them as principles with no further explanations.

The considerations above direct to different ways. Since postulates are at a different level from the norms subject to application, defining them as principles or rules would confuse more than explain. Besides that, postulates work very differently from principles and rules. Truly, principles are defined as immediately finalistic norms, i.e., norms that impose the advancement of an ideal state of affairs by indirectly describing behaviors whose effects are seen as necessary for that advancement. Differently, postulates, on the one hand, do not impose the advancement of a goal, rather they scaffold the application of the duty to advance a goal; on the other hand, they do not indirectly describe behaviors, but lines of thinking and arguing regarding norms that indirectly describe behaviors. Strictly speaking, then, principles and postulates are not to be confused.

On their turn, rules are norms immediately describing due behaviors or assigning power. Differently, postulates do not describe behaviors, but scaffold the application of the rules that do so. Even if rules were defined as norms that set forth, forbid or allow what is to be done, their consequences being bound to be implemented with the occurrence of their conditions, as DWORKIN and ALEXY do, still the complexity of postulates would withdraw from this dual model. The analysis of the postulates of reasonableness and proportionality, for instance, are far from requiring a mere coupling activity from judges. Instead, they require sorting through and relating several elements (means and end, criterion and measure, general rule and individual case), and not a mere assessment of the correspondence between the norm conditions and the factual elements. The possibility of eventually requiring the whole application does not rule out different usage in preparing the decision. Principles, too, at the end of the application process, require whole fulfilling. And the circumstance of all normative species ultimately focusing on human behavior does not rule out the importance of explaining the completely different proceedings that prepare and justify what is unearthed.

The difficulties of classifying proportionality, for instance, as rules and principles, are evident in the very conceptions of those that place it under such categories. Even those who understand what we call normative applicative postulates as second level rules acknowledge that, as the optimization commands, they are *a specific form of rules* (*eine besondere Form von Regeln*).[31] The ones who understand them as principles also acknowledge that they operate as a maxim or argumentative reference that combines the features of rules and those of principles.[32] Others argue soundly to classify them as particular principles, called legitimization principles.[33] And there are still others that present them as methodical rules.[34]

These considerations make believe that these duties deserve a particular definition and, consequently, a different denomination. This work calls them normative applicative postulates. The name is of secondary importance. What is fundamental is to verify and justify its different mode of operation.

3.4. CONSEQUENCES OF THE INCONSISTENT USE OF NORMS AND METANORMS

Second degree norms, redefined as applied normative postulates, are different from rules and principles because of their level and their function. Whereas principles and rules are the object under application, postulates set forth the application criteria of principles and rules. And whereas principles and rules work as commands to identify mandatory, allowed, and forbidden conducts, or conducts whose adoption is required for the realization of certain goals, postulates provide parameters for the realization of other norms.

Every time postulates are used, there is always reasoning regarding the application of other norms of the legal order. As will be discussed further on, when reasonableness-equivalence is examined, norms are analyzed that establish the intervention or act with the goal of identifying whether there is an equivalence between its dimension and that which it aims to punish or promote. In the exam of proportionality, norms are examined that establish the intervention or act that identifies whether the principle that justifies its creation will be promoted and the extent to which other principles will be restricted. In the examination of prohibition of excess, norms are analyzed that establish the intervention or act that checks whether any fundamental principle is being attacked in its core. Therefore arises the question of learning whether there is an excessive restriction of fundamental principles.

This shows that these exams investigate how norms ought to be applied to other norms, either by establishing criteria, or by defining measures. In any case, the requirements stemming from reasonableness, proportionality and prohibition of excess converge onto other norms, not to assign them meaning, though, but to structure their application rationally. There is always another norm behind the application of reasonableness, proportionality and excessiveness. This is the reason why it is appropriate to treat them as metanorms. And since they structure the application of other norms, but are not the same as these, it is appropriate to refer to them under a different name. Therefore the use of the term "postulate" to refer to a norm that structures the application of others.

However, the requirements of proportionality, reasonableness and prohibition of excess are usually defined as principles. Still, they cannot be principles, either under the weak distinction or under the strong distinction between normative species.

In case one accepts the weak distinction between principles and rules, proportionality, for example, cannot be considered an instance of principle because it does not have a high degree of abstraction and generality: it is aimed to certain situations (collision between principles due to the use of a means whose adoption causes effects that promote the realization of a principle, but restrict the realization of another) and to certain people (individuals, usually public authorities, who adopt measures with the intention of realizing certain principles). It cannot be considered as a rule, either, because it does not have a hypothesis and a consequence that allows the coupling of the factual concept to the norm concept. Instead of a factual hypothesis or an effect definition, proportionality sets forth an application structure, which is something quite different.

In case one accepts the strong distinction between principles and rules, proportionality, for example, cannot be considered an instance of principle, either, because it is not realized in several degrees, but in a single one (either the measure is appropriate or not, either it is necessary or not) and because it is not the object of counterbalancing, but its criterion. It is inconceivable to outweigh it because of horizontally colliding principles. Likewise, it cannot be considered a rule because it does not have a hypotheses and a consequence to be enforced in case of coupling. Neither can it collide or be declared non-valid.

The definition of second degree applied norms as principles or rules is less a matter of naming than it is a circumstantial matter of coherence and justification.

It is a circumstantial matter because, if there are two circumstances to consider, why call them the same name? There is no reason to do so. It belittles language by not making use of it.

It is a matter of coherence because not only authors who use the weak criterion (principles are more general and abstract norms, and rules are less general and abstract) but also those who use the strong criterion (principles are optimization norms that are realizable in several degrees, and rules are norms that set forth a hypothesis and a defining commandment) could not define proportionality, for example, as a principle or as a rule and keep their scientific coherence. Not as a principle, because it is not realized in several degrees – it is the criterion for the realization in several degrees of the goals whose promotion is due because of the enactment of principles. And not as a rule, either, because it does not have a hypothesis and a consequence, neither can it be excluded from the legal order in case of a collision.

Finally, it is a matter of justification, because a definition of proportionality as a principle/rule will confuse the object of the application and the criterion of application. One could think of it as a metaphor: the definition of proportionality as a principle mixes up the scales with the objects it weighs! And, in doing it, one loses sight of the difference between that which is to be realized (principles/rules) and that which is the parameter for their realization (postulates).

3.5. GUIDELINES TO ANALYZE NORMATIVE APPLICATIVE POSTULATES

Given the definition of postulates as structuring norms of application of principles and rules, the following steps are proposed to investigate it.

1st The need to collect cases where the solution was based on a normative postulate.

The investigation of normative postulates begins with the analysis of precedents. Cases ought to be found that were resolved by applying the postulates under analysis. The importance of proportionality and reasonableness, for instance, grows day by day in Brazilian Case Law. High court decisions that use it are not few.

In concrete terms, it means: (a) to investigate the precedents of Higher Courts in search of opinions that have mentioned the use of normative postulates; (b) to obtain the full text of the opinions that refer such postulates.

2nd An analysis of the justification of said opinions in order to verify the elements listed and the way they have been interrelated.

After that, it is necessary to analyze the justification of the decisions with the aim of finding which elements were listed and how they were related to one another. As mentioned earlier, normative postulates scaffold the application of other norms. Therefore, it is indispensable to verify which norms were applied, and how. For instance, the postulate of reasonableness is used to apply equality, to demand a relation of congruence between a distinctive criterion and the discriminatory measure. An examination of the decision shows there are two elements under analysis, criterion and measure, and a certain relation of congruence is required between them.

Specifically, that means: (a) to analyze decisions and to verify the elements or magnitudes that have been manipulated; (b) to explore which relations are considered essential between them.

3rd Investigation of norms that were applied and justification for choosing some application.

Since postulates are duties that scaffold the application of legal norms, it is important to examine not only which norms have been applied but also the justification of the decision. For example, the postulate of proportionality requires all measures taken by the government to be appropriate, necessary and proportional in a strict sense. In the case where the Supreme Court ruled out as unconstitutional a state statute that provided for the use of a special scale to weigh gas bottles in front of consumers, the Court analyzed the means used (order to use scales), the purpose aimed at (principle of consumer protection) and the collaterally restricted principle (principle of free initiative). As can be inferred from reading the entire opinion, the petitioner alleged that the means was not totally appropriate to advance the purpose (according to an opinion of the National Institute of Measurements — INMETRO, the scales were inappropriate to measure the content of the containers because the use of manometers did not meet the required purpose, since liquified petroleum gas is measured in units of mass and not units of pressure), other less restrictive means could have been chosen (seals, night watch) and the disadvantages (expenses to buy scales, transfer of costs to the price of containers, need to have consumer go to the transporting vehicle) overcame the advantages (greater control of content of containers, protection of consumers' trust).[35] In short, an examination of the opinion of the court lets one identify the elements under analysis and the relations required among them.

In details, it means: (a) to verify the elements or magnitudes that have been manipulated; (b) to find the reasons that made judges understand certain interrelations as existent or non-existent.

4th Trailing the way backwards: having found the structure required to apply the postulate, verify the existence of other cases that should have been decided according to them.

The first step to examine postulates, as already referred, is to analyze the decisions that have used them expressly. There are cases, however, where a given postulate is used without express mention to it. In other cases, although the elements are present along with the duty to define the specific relation among them, the postulate is not used. In others yet, there is express mention to a postulate, but the elements and their relations are different from the elements and the relations that exist in decisions supposedly based on the same postulate. Given all that, after identifying situations of typical application of postulates, it is necessary to search anew. This time, the focus is not on the postulate as a keyword, but on the search for the elements and relations that support its application.

To put it simply, that means: (a) to search precedents again, looking for other keywords; (b) to analyze the decisions found critically, rebuilding them argumentatively according to the postulate under exam so as to evidence non-use or misuse.

3.6. SPECIES OF POSTULATES

3.6.1. General Aspects

Normative postulates have been defined as structuring duties, i.e., duties that establish a bond between *elements* and impose a certain *relation* between them. In that, they can be considered formal, since they depend on a combination of substantive reasons to be applied.

Postulates do not all operate the same way. Some can be applied regardless of the elements subject to interrelation. As will be seen, weighing requires counterbalancing any elements (goods, interests, values, rights, principles, reasons) and does not show how to counterbalance. The elements and criteria are not specific. Practical accordance operates similarly: the harmonization of elements is required, but their species is not mentioned. The elements to be harmonized are indeterminate. The prohibition of excess also ordains that the realization of one element can not cause the annihilation of another. The elements to be minimally preserved are not pointed. Likewise, the postulate of optimization establishes that certain elements ought to be maximized without stating which or how.

In these cases, normative postulates require relations between elements without specifying which elements and criteria should guide their relation, though. Such normative postulates are mostly formal. Hence, they are mere general ideas, void of guiding application criteria[36], which is why they are herein called nonspecific (or unconditional) postulates.

The application of other postulates depends on the existence of some elements and it is defined by certain criteria. Equality is only applicable in situations where there is a relation between two or more subjects due to a differentiating criterion that serves some purpose. Its applicability is dependent on the existence of specific elements (subjects, differentiating criterion and purpose). Reasonableness is only applicable where there is a conflict between general and individual, between a norm and the reality it regulates and between a criterion and a measure. Its applicability is dependent on the existence of specific elements (general and individual, norm and reality, criterion and measure). Proportionality is only applicable where there is causation between means and purpose. Its applicability is dependent on the existence of specific elements (means and purpose).

In these cases, normative postulates require a relation between specific elements, and criteria to guide their relation. They are formal normative postulates, too, but they refer to elements of determined species, which is why they are also herein called specific (or conditional) postulates.

3.6.2. Nonspecific Postulates

3.6.2.1. Weighing *Weighing legal goods* (Rechtsgüter) is a method of assigning weights to entangling elements without referring to substantive points of view that guide this counterbalance. Here and there, one can hear about weighing assets, values, principles, purposes, interests. Within the scope of this study, it is important to point out that weighing without substantive criteria and structure is of very little use to Law. Weighing ought to be structured with criteria.[37] That becomes clear when it is observed that studies on this matter invariably attempt to structure it with postulates of reasonableness and proportionality and guide it by using fundamental constitutional principles. In that aspect, weighing, as a mere method or general idea void of substantive or formal criteria, is much broader than the postulates of proportionality and reasonableness.[38]

It also involves being aware of the importance of distinguishing the elements subject to weighing, which, however interrelated, can be distinguished. *Legal goods* are situations, states or qualities essential to the promotion of legal principles.[39] For instance, the principle of free initiative presupposes free agency and autonomy as conditions for its accomplishment. Freedom and autonomy are legal goods protected by the principle of free initiative. *Interests* are the very legal assets in their connection with a given subject seeking to obtain it. For instance, freedom and autonomy being legal goods protected by the principle of free initiative, a certain person may have – given certain circumstances – conditions to enjoy that freedom and autonomy. Freedom and autonomy thus become part of the interests of such person. *Values* comprise the axiological aspect of norms, as they manifest that something is good and therefore worthy of being sought or preserved.[40] From that perspective, freedom is a value and therefore ought to be sought or preserved. *Principles* comprise the deontological aspect of values because they not only demonstrate something worth seeking but also determine that such state of affairs ought to be promoted.

When the expression "weighing" is used, all elements above are worthy of being counterweighed. What matters, however, is to know the subtle difference between them. Clarity will be rewarded.

However, despite the elements counterbalanced, one can evolve to an intensely structured balancing, which can be used to apply specific postulates. In order to achieve that, some stages are fundamental.[41]

The first stage is to *prepare to weigh* (*Abwägungsvorbereitung*). In this stage, all elements and arguments ought to be analyzed as exhaustively as possible.[42] It is usual to start weighing without pointing out beforehand what is being weighed. Obviously, that violates the scientific postulate of explicitness of premises as well as the legal principle of justifying decisions, innate to the Rule of Law.

The second stage is that of *performing the counterbalance* (*Abwägung*), where the relation found between the counterweighed elements will be justified. Where principles are weighed, this stage indicates which takes precedence to the other.

The third stage is to *rebuild counterbalance* (*Rekonstruktion der Abwägung*), by formulating relation rules, including those of precedence among the counterweighed elements, expecting them to be valid beyond the case.

Counterweighing criteria can be many. Special attention should be given to constitutional principles and the argumentation rules construed from them, such as that according to which linguistic and systematic arguments must take precedence over historical, genetic and merely pragmatic ones.[43]

3.6.2.2. Practical accordance Within this context, practical accordance appears as the guiding purpose of counterweighing: the duty of achieving juxtaposing values to their maximum extent. This postulate arises from the coexistence of values that totally or partially point to opposed directions. Therefrom comes the duty of harmonizing values so that they are protected to their most. As there is tension between constitutional rules and principles, notably between those that protect citizens and those that grant powers to the state, a balance between them ought to be sought. Regarding that, DÜRIG mentions the duty to find out a *dialectic synthesis* between the juxtaposed norms in order to find an optimization of the conflicting values.[44]

Neither weighing nor practical accordance, however, show the formal or substantive criteria through which the entangled purposes are to be promoted. Structures are formed that are exclusively formal and void of criteria. As will be investigated later on, it is the postulates of reasonableness and proportionality that allowed structuring the realization of the constitutional norms.

3.6.2.3. Prohibition of excess However, there is a limit to the promotion of constitutional purposes. This limit is given by the postulate of prohibition of excess. Oftentimes called a facet of the principle of proportionality by the Supreme Court, the postulate of prohibition of excess prohibits the excessive restriction of any fundamental right.

The prohibition of excess is present in any situation where a fundamental right is under restriction. Therefore, it ought to be investigated apart from the postulate of proportionality: applying it does not presuppose the existence of causation between means and end. The postulate of prohibition of excess depends exclusively on a fundamental right being excessively restricted.

The realization of a constitutional principle or rule cannot lead to restricting a fundamental right so as to make it void of efficacy. For instance, the power to tax cannot annihilate free initiative. In such case, counterbalancing values shows that applying a norm, rule or principle (the State jurisdiction to create taxes) cannot lead to the impossibility of applying another norm, rule or principle (the protection of private property).[45] Some cases may clarify the matter better.

The Second Bench of the Supreme Court turned down an appeal because it understood it was excessive and disproportional to increase the license tax of bathing cabins. Petitioner argued that such levy could forbid it from keeping a licit activity, which would collide with the principle of freedom of professional activity (art. 141, §14 of the 1946 Constitution).[46] The opinion of Justice Orozimbo Nonato quotes a decision of the Supreme Court of the United States that *"the power to tax is to be exercised only within limits that make it compatible with the freedom of work, trade and industry, and with the right of property."* Therefore, despite considering the tax *"immoderate"*, the Justice acknowledged it to be due, because it did not *"annihilate private activity,"* which would be key to identify excess in the tax increase.

In another decision, the Full Bench of the Supreme Court granted a preliminary injunction based on the unconstitutionality of a State statute that increased the amount of legal fees. Such State Statute would be *"in violation of arts. 153, §§30 and 32; art. 19, I; and art. 8º, XVII, 'c' "* of the Constitution then in force.[47] Because court fees were raised by 827%, a large portion of the population would not have access to the Judiciary system. The opinion of the Court accepted petitioner's arguments and pleaded for the need to protect a public interest (access to legal services) besides arguing that there was the harm of irreparable damage should the injunction be denied.

In another case, the First Bench of the Supreme Court reversed in part a lower instance court decision that ordered payment of *"Seal Tax in loans recorded under checking accounts without written contracts, according to article 49 of the Table attached to the Seal Regulations (Executive Law 4655/42)."* The lower court decision also sustained a fine for not paying the tax which equaled fifty times the price of the seal. The Supreme Court affirmed the right to collect the Seal Tax, but reversed the part regarding the fine as excessive.[48]

In all of these cases, the Supreme Court did not investigate the legitimacy of the purpose, nor the need to embrace those measures, neither the presence of public interests that might justify such measures. Appropriateness, necessity and proportionality were not examined in their strict meaning because of a relation between means and end. Instead, the Court only perceived that no measure can restrict a fundamental right excessively, whatever the reason to justify it. Therefore the prohibition of excess is spoken of as a limit apart from the postulate of proportionality.[49]

Besides that, it is plausible to imagine cases where the governmental measure is considered disproportional without being considered excessive.

Let us examine an example. In order to protect consumers, the government orders supermarkets of some region to label all products sold in their stores. The measure is the means to accomplish a purpose, which is consumer protection. The adoption of the measure restrains the free exercise of economic activity by the supermarkets. Since the situation involves causation of means and a real purpose, the postulate of proportionality is applicable. Upon examining appropriateness, it is concluded that the effects of the measure do contribute to a gradual realization of the purpose. Labeling products does contribute to consumer protection. Examining necessity, it is plausible to decide there is no alternate way if the available methods are not considered equally appropriate to protect consumers. The effects of implementing bar codes promote consumer protection less intensely than labeling each product. The obligation of labeling products is necessary. Counterbalancing the advantages and disadvantages of the measure, it can be concluded that although there is not any other equally appropriate means to protect consumers, still the *level of restriction* to the free exercise of economic activity (administrative costs, labor to label and then re-label when prices change, transfer of costs to product prices, abandoning a modern system of bar coding) is disproportional to the level of promotion of the principle of consumer protection (protection of an inadvertent minority of consumers in detriment of the average consumer who is already protected by other existing means). Therefore, the measure, though appropriate and necessary, is considered disproportional in a strict sense.

Regardless of the merits of the proposed solution, the example is helpful in showing that the three exams inherent to proportionality (appropriateness, necessity and proportionality) were carried out and at no time was it theorized to restrict the essential core of the free exercise of economic activities. Supermarkets will not go bankrupt, their freedoms as a whole will not be annihilated and, still, the measure was considered disproportional. That is to say: the measure was considered disproportional without being excessive in the sense of invading the inviolable core of fundamental rights. That means, in short, that it is possible to examine with the postulate of proportionality without any control with the postulate of prohibition of excess. And it is possible to examine with the postulate of prohibition of excess without control with the postulate of proportionality, as is the case, for instance, of the aforementioned cases of taxation with fiscal purposes, where there is no causation between means and a concrete purpose, and still the adopted measures were considered excessive. Hence, they are distinct postulates because they are applied distinctly.

In order to understand the distinction between the postulate of proportionality and the postulate of prohibition of excess, one needs to observe that the latter operates at a level *from which* the essential core of the restrained fundamental principle is preserved. In a graphical sense, we could imagine a large circle that represented the degrees of restriction of a fundamental principle of freedom, inside of which other smaller, concentric circles are inserted until they arrive at the smallest central circle which represents the inviolable core. Public purposes could justify a restriction placed between the most external and the most internal ring, where trespassing is forbidden. Hence, the postulate of proportionality in a narrow sense operates between the limits of the innermost and outermost rings and compares the level of restriction of freedom with the level of promotion of public purposes in order to declare as invalid a measure that restrains *too much* to promote *too little*. For the sake of comprehension, it would be like saying that promoting a level "one" public purpose does not justify restricting a level "four" fundamental principle. Such measure, in this case, would be disproportional in a narrow sense. The prohibition of excess would supposedly indicate that no restriction could be equivalent to level five, which would represent the forbidden central ring, regardless of its justification and degree of realization.

All of these considerations, whose understanding requires quite a bit of imagination, aim only at showing that the control method required by the prohibition of excess is different from that required by the postulate of proportionality. The control structure being different, clarity seekers are led to adopt words that are also different. Such structures — let us say it over and over — can be explained differently and use the same names. That is one thing. What can not be done — let it be stressed again and again — is to mix them up by using the same name. That is something else.

3.6.3. *Specific Postulates*

3.6.3.1. Equality Equality can operate as a rule, providing for the prohibition of discriminatory treatment; as a principle, setting forth an egalitarian state as a goal to be accomplished; and as a postulate, structuring the application of the Law in terms of elements (criterion of differentiation and purpose of distinction) and their interrelation (congruence of criterion in respect of the purpose).

The realization of the principle of equality depends on the criterion-measure that is subject to differentiation.[50] This is so because the principle of equality, in itself, says nothing about the assets or purposes that equality uses to discern or compare people. People or situations are equal or unequal due to some differentiating criterion. Two people are formally equal or different due to age, sex or economic capacity. This differentiation only takes up some *substantive* importance as a purpose is aggregated, so that people become equal or different according to a common criterion, depending on the purpose it serves. Two people may be equal or different according to the *criterion of age*: they ought to be treated differently for voting in a given election if one has become of age and the other has not; they ought to be treated equally for paying taxes because this goal is realized regardless of age. Two people may be considered equal or different according to the *criterion of gender*: they ought to be seen differently in order to obtain a maternity leave if only one of them is female; they ought to be treated equally for voting or paying taxes because these goals are realized regardless of sex. Likewise, two people may be considered equal or different according to the *criterion of economic capacity*: they ought to be seen differently to pay taxes if one has greater tax paying capacity; they are treated equally for voting and obtaining a maternity leave because the economic capacity is neutral to the realization of these purposes.[51]

It is worth saying that the application of equality depends on a *differentiating criterion* and on a *purpose* to be achieved. That observation leads to an equally important and neglected conclusion: different purposes cause the utilization of different criteria because of a simple reason: some criteria are appropriate to realize some purposes while others are not. More than that: several purposes lead to different control measures. Law has purposes and purposes.[52] As a postulate, its violation leads back to the violation of some legal norm. Subjects ought to be considered equal in freedom, property and dignity. Violating equality implies the violation of a fundamental principle.

3.6.3.2. Reasonableness

3.6.3.2.1. Overview

Reasonableness scaffolds the application of other norms, principles and rules, mainly rules. Reasonableness is used in several senses. One can read about reasonableness of an allegation, reasonableness of an interpretation, reasonableness of a restriction, reasonableness of a statutory goal, reasonableness of a legislative function.[53] In short, reasonableness is used in several contexts and for several purposes. Although the decisions of Higher Courts do not use terms uniformly nor use explicit and clear criteria to justify the postulates of proportionality and reasonableness, it is still possible — and anyway this is one of the purposes of Jurisprudence — to rebuild decisions analytically, thus conferring them their expected clarity. For that reason, it can not be said that their lack of express use of criteria in examining proportionality and reasonableness keeps law scholars from analytically reconstruing decisions and learning which criteria are implicitly used in Supreme Court case law.[54]

Regarding reasonableness, three conceptions stand out among many. First of all, reasonableness is used as a guideline that requires general norms to be related with individualities in real cases, either showing from which perspective the norm should be applied or indicating in which situation the individual case is so specific it does not conform to the general norm. Secondly, reasonableness is used as a guideline that requires legal norms to be related to the world they refer, either by demanding an empirical and appropriate support to any legal act or by demanding a congruent relation between the adopted measure and the purpose it expects to accomplish. Thirdly, reasonableness is used as a guideline that requires a relation of equivalence between two magnitudes. These are the conceptions investigated from now on.

3.6.3.2.2. Concepts

3.6.3.2.2.1. Reasonableness as fairness

In the first group of cases, the postulate of reasonableness requires the harmonization of the general rule and the individual case.

First of all, reasonableness compels an understanding of what commonly happens for legal norms to be applied. A few cases may illustrate this requirement.

A criminal lawyer requested the court to postpone trial before a jury because he was working on another controversial case that would be tried at about the same time. His first plead was granted. After advocating for his client, and having the recommendation to rest for two weeks, the lawyer repeated his request. This time, the judge overruled it because he understood that it was insulting to Justice, assuming that the lawyer was maliciously trying to put off the trial. On the date set for trial, even after the defendant stated that his lawyer was not present, the Presiding Judge appointed a lawyer, who took over the defense. Unsatisfied with the denial to his request and with the very outcome of the trial, the lawyer filed a writ of habeas corpus. The decision stated that it did not seem unreasonable that that lawyer, who argued complex cases which were happening quite frequently, might request for an extension of time due to what happened in the previous trial. In short, it was set that it is reasonable to assume that people tell the truth and act in good faith, rather than lie and act in malice. In applying the Law, what usually happens ought to be assumed, and not the contrary. The defense of the appointed lawyer was annulled because the overruling of the lawyer's request for postponement restricted the defendant's *right to defense*.[55]

A State Attorney who filed an appeal on stationery of the State Department of Legal Affairs was required to prove his position by presenting evidence that he had taken office or a document from the Attorney General of the State. Upon the allegation of lack of power of attorney, the matter was tried and it was decided that power of attorney can be presumed when the attorney is exercising statutory powers. When statutory norms are interpreted, one ought to assume what usually happens, and not the contrary, such as someone pretending to be a State Attorney without actually being one. Because of that, a higher court determined that the appeal be received because denying it directly affected the right to *extensive defense* only because of an extreme fondness of formalities.[56]

Power of attorney signed by a representative of the government who mentions the position held within the structure of the Administration can not be considered irregular or false. When interpreting norms, one ought to assume what happens daily, not extraordinarily.[57]

In the cases above, reasonableness is a tool to determine the factual circumstances ought to be assumed as within normalcy. Reasonableness operates on the interpretation of facts described in legal rules. Reasonableness requires some interpretation as the means to preserve the efficacy of axiologically overlying principles. A different interpretation from the factual circumstances would cause a constitutional principle to be restricted, such as the principle of the due process of law, in the studied cases.

Secondly, reasonableness requires the individual aspect of the case to be taken into account where the statutory generalization disregards it exceedingly. In some cases, because of specific reasons, the general norm can not be applicable because the case is unusual. A previously mentioned example illustrates that duty.

A small sofa factory, classified as small for the purpose of unified payment of federal taxes, was excluded from this scheme for violating the statutory restriction of not importing foreign products. True, the company did import. However, it only imported four legs for a single sofa, only once. On appeal, the exclusion was reversed for violating reasonableness, since a *reasonable interpretation* indicates that the interpretation ought to be "in accordance with what common sense would find legally acceptable."[58] In this case, the condition was met according to which imports are prohibited for permanence in that special taxation scheme, but the consequence for not complying with it was not applied (exclusion from the special taxation scheme) because not following the behavior the rule set forth did not harm the promotion of the purpose it justified (to stimulate small companies to manufacture nationally). In other words, according to the decision, national production would still not be harmed if a few legs for a sofa were imported.

In the case above, the general rule which applies to cases in general was not found applicable to an individual case because it is so distinct. Not all norms are applied when conditions are met. It is necessary to set apart the applicability of a rule from the satisfaction of its hypothetical conditions. A rule is not applicable just because its operative facts occur. A rule applies to a case if and only if its operative facts occur and application is not excluded by the reason that justifies the rule itself or by the existence of a principle that sets forth a contrary reason. In these cases, the conditions of applicability are met, but the rule is not applied anyway.[59] In the cases under analysis, the conditions for application of the rules were met. In the first case, the condition was met according to which taking a public office requires a public contest, because the matter was about a public career and taking office. Still, the rule was not applied: it was understood that the rule was not violated *in that case*. In the second case, the condition of the rule, according to which a taxpayer ought to be excluded from a special tax-paying system when it imports, was met. Still, the rule was not applied: the taxpayer was not excluded *in that case*. The concept of reasonableness matches the teachings of ARISTOTLE, who sees fairness as a remedy for the law when and where it is deficient for being general.[60]

These considerations lead to the conclusion that reasonableness is a methodological tool to tell that the occurrence of operative facts is a necessary but insufficient step to apply a rule. To make it applicable, the real case must adapt to the generality of the general norm. Reasonableness operates on the interpretation of general rules as a consequence of the principle of Justice (introduction and third article of the Federal Constitution).

3.6.3.2.2.2. Reasonableness as congruence

In the second group of cases, the postulate of reasonableness requires the harmonization of norms and the external conditions of application.

Firstly, reasonableness requires referring to an existing empirical support for any measure.[61] Some examples prove it.

A state statute created an additional vacation payment of a third of the regular salary for retired workers. Upon judgment, the additional payment was overruled because it represented a benefit *without a cause* and without the amount of reason enough, since only workers who have vacation should have an additional vacation payment. Consequently, the creation was annulled because it violated the due process of law, which is a decisive check on unreasonable and arbitrary acts of the legislative.[62]

A state statute ordered that schools issue certificates of course conclusion and school reports to high school third-graders who proved admission to a college or university, regardless of the number of classes attended, in time for students to enroll in the courses they had been admitted to. The Supreme Court found it legally relevant to examine the constitutionality Petitioner argued against because such statute, at first sight, seems to be void of reasonableness as it *inverts the natural order* of schooling by granting students the right to have conclusion certificates issued regardless of attendance as long as word of admission had been given.[63]

A norm in a State Constitution established that public servants were to be paid on the tenth working day of each month, with no delay. The Supreme Court found it unreasonable that the disputed norm, in order to avoid such delays, ordered prepayment for *services that had not been rendered yet*.[64]

In these cases, legislators choose an inexistent or insufficient cause for state action. In doing so, they violate the requirement of connection with reality.[65] Interpreting norms requires their confrontation with external parameters. Therefore it is spoken of congruence and justification based on the nature of things (*Natur der Sache*). The constitutional principles of the rule of law (article first) and due process of law (article fifth, item LIV), prevent the use of arbitrary reasons and the subversion of institutional proceedings used. Disengaging from reality is violating the principles of the rule of law and due process of law.

This requirement is also important in the cases of anachronic legislation, i.e., those cases where the norm was conceived for application in a certain socioeconomic context which is no longer applicable.[66]

Secondly, reasonableness requires a congruent relation between the criterion of differentiation chosen and the adopted measure.[67] An analysis of some cases can show that.

The Executive issued a provisional measure with the purpose of extending the statute of limitations from two to five years for the Federal and State governments, and Municipalities, to file a motion for new trial. Upon judgment, it was averred that the Public Power does have some prerogatives; however, these are to be based on actual differences between the parties and not only become a hindrance to the satisfaction of private citizen's rights. Only a plausible and acceptable reason justifies the distinction. Because of that and other motivations, the provisional measure was ruled unconstitutional because the creation of arbitrary discrimination violates the principles of equality and due process of law.[68]

A state statute determined that the labor time of Secretaries of State should be counted double for effects of retirement. Upon judgment, it was decided that it is not reasonable to understand that the labor time of a Secretary of State is worth double that of other public servants. This is arbitrary or random discrimination. Because of that, the distinction was ruled invalid, since creating distinctions without a cause violates the principle of equality.[69]

A statute linked the number of candidates in a political party to the number of seats of each State in the House of Representatives. The number of candidates was pointed as a means of electoral discrimination. The parties appealed, calling the statute unreasonable. It was ruled, however, that the distinction criterion and the adopted measure were congruent, because linking the number of seats to the number of candidates would lead to better representation of the population.[70]

In the three cases mentioned above, the postulate of reasonableness required a correlation between the distinctive criterion the norm used and the measure it adopted. What is under analysis here is not the relation between means and purpose, but that between criterion and measure. The efficacy of the constitutional principles of the rule of law (article first) and due process of law (article fifth, item LIV) is joined to the efficacy of the principle of equality (article fifth, head), which prevents the use of inappropriate distinctive criteria. Differentiating without a reason is violating the principle of equality.

3.6.3.2.2.3. Reasonableness as equivalence

Reasonableness also requires a relation of equivalence between the adopted measure and the criterion that gives its dimension.

The Supreme Court found it unconstitutional to create a court fee with an across-the-board rate because it believed that in some cases this tax would be so high as to prevent the exercise of a fundamental right — access to court services — besides not being *reasonably* equivalent to the actual cost of the service.[71] In this case, the decision is founded on the matter relating the prohibition of excess, but also on the lack of proportionality between the cost of service and the fee charged. Service fees are to be set according to the service rendered or offered to the taxpayer. Therefore, the cost of the service is a guide to the calculation of the fees. Hence, it is said that fees ought to be *equivalent* to the service rendered.

Another example regards the penalties to be set according to the actor's culpability. In this case, fault is a criterion to determine the sentence to be served, and the sentence matches the fault. The Supreme Court, in a case mentioned previously, decided to block a criminal action for lack of probable cause once it verified the supposedly criminal act was legally trifling. It is a trifle for a city to hire a single worker to sweep streets for a short period of time; the pleadings in a labor complaint were overruled because the legal relation was null due to the lack of public contest. The punishment would not be *equivalent* to the criminal act.[72]

3.6.3.2.2.4. Distinction between reasonableness and proportionality

The postulate of proportionality requires that the Legislative and the Executive choose appropriate, necessary and proportional means in order to achieve their purposes. A means is appropriate if it promote the purpose. It is necessary if, among all other equally appropriate means to promote the purpose, it is the least restrictive regarding fundamental rights. And it is proportional, in a narrow sense, if the advantages it promotes are superior to the disadvantages it causes. The application of proportionality requires the relation of causation between means and purpose so that the adoption of the means promotes the purpose.[73]

What happens is that reasonableness, reconstructed as proposed here, does not refer a relation of cause between *means* and *purpose*, such as the postulate of proportionality. This is shown hereafter.

Reasonableness as a duty of harmonization between the general and the individual (a duty of equity) operates as an instrument to determine that circumstances of fact ought to be considered presumably within normality or to express that the applicability of the general rule depends on the conformance of the concrete case. In these cases, overlying constitutional principles vertically impose a given interpretation. However, there is no horizontal crossing of principles nor relation of causation between means and a purpose. There is no space to state that an action promotes the realization of a state of affairs.

Reasonableness as a duty of harmonization of the Law and its external conditions (duty of congruence) requires relating norms and their external conditions of application, either by demanding an existent empirical support to adopt a measure, or by demanding a congruent relation between the chosen criterion of differentiation and the adopted measure.

In the first case, overlying constitutional principles vertically impose one interpretation by repelling arbitrary reason. There is not any horizontal crossing of principles nor relation of causation between means and purpose.

In the second case, a correlation is required between the distinctive criterion the norm uses and the measure it adopts. The relation under analysis here is not the one between means and ends, but that between criterion and measure. Truly, the postulate of proportionality presupposes causation between the effect of an action (means) and the promotion of a state of affairs (purpose). By adopting the means, the purpose is furthered: the means leads to the purpose. On the other hand, when reasonableness is the congruence requirement between the chosen criterion of differentiation and the adopted measure, there is a relation between a quality and an adopted measure: a quality does not lead to the measure; rather, it is part of it.

Reasonableness as a duty of connection between two magnitudes (duty of equivalence), like the congruence requirement, imposes a relation of equivalence between the adopted measure and the criterion that *gives its dimension*. In this case, a relation between criterion and measure is required, and not between means and purpose. This is so much so that one can not maintain, for the cases under analysis, that the cost of the service furthers the fee, or that fault leads to the penalty. In these cases there is not any causation between two empirically different elements, a means and a purpose, as is the case of the application of the principle of proportionality. There is, however, a matching relationship between two *magnitudes*.[74]

Even though this is not the alternative chosen for this work for reasons already mentioned, it is plausible to conform the prohibition of excess and reasonableness into the exam of proportionality in a narrow sense. If proportionality is understood, in a strict sense, as a broad duty of weighing assets, principles and values where the advancement of one cannot imply the annihilation of another, the prohibition of excess will be included in the exam of proportionality.[75] If proportionality, in a strict sense, comprises weighing several conflicting interests, including the personal interest of the owners of the restricted fundamental rights, reasonableness as fairness will be included in the exam of proportionality.[76] That means that the same theoretical problem can be analyzed from different viewpoints and with distinct purposes, all of them equally dignified in theory. Therefore, it cannot be stated that one or another way to explain proportionality is correct and others are wrong.[77]

3.6.3.3. *Proportionality*

3.6.3.3.1. General overview

The postulate of proportionality has been growing in importance in Brazilian Law. More and more, it works as a tool to control acts of the government.[78] Naturally, its application has caused several problems.

The first one of them regards its applicability. Its roots can be traced to the use of the word *proportion* itself. The notion of *proportion* is recurrent in Jurisprudence. In the General Theory of Law proportion is quoted as an element of the very immemorial concept of Law, which serves to give each one a proportional share. In Criminal Law, one refers to the need of proportion between guilt and punishment when defining the latter. In Election Law, one refers the proportion between the number of candidates and the number of seats as a condition to assess representativeness. In Tax Law, one mentions the mandatory proportion between the amount of tax and the public service rendered and the need of proportion between the tax burden and the public services the State offers society. In Procedural Law, one exploits the idea of proportion between the burden caused and the purpose of the procedural act. In Constitutional and Administrative Law, one uses the notion of proportion between the burden an act of the government creates and the purpose it pursues. And, in assessing the force of the burden caused, one talks about the proportion between advantages and disadvantages, between pros and cons, between restraining a right and advancing a purpose and so on. The notion of proportion permeates all the Law without limits or criteria.

However, are all of these notions about the postulate of proportionality? Certainly not. The postulate of proportionality is not to be mistaken for the notion of proportion in its various instances. It is applicable only to situations where there is causation between two empirically discernible elements, a means and a purpose, so much so that three fundamental exams can proceed: appropriateness (does the means promote the purpose?), necessity (among the means available and equally appropriate to further the purpose, is not there one less restrictive of the fundamental right or rights at stake?), and proportionality in a narrow sense (do the advantages of promoting the purpose match the disadvantages of adopting the means?).

In this sense, proportionality, as a postulate that scaffolds the application of principles that actually juxtapose around a relation of causation between a means and a purpose, is not applicable without restrictions. Its application depends on elements without which it cannot be applied. Without means, a real purpose and a relation of causation between them, the postulate of proportionality is not applicable in its three-phased aspect.

The second problem regards its operation. Apparently it is clear that the postulate of proportionality requires the exams of appropriateness, necessity and proportionality in a narrow sense. The means ought to be appropriate to accomplish the purpose. However, what exactly is *appropriateness*? The means chosen from those available ought to be necessary. However, what does it mean do be *necessary*? The advantages of using the means must overthrow the disadvantages. But what is an *advantage* and *what* and *who* does it compare to? Hence, the three exams of proportionality are uncontroversial only apparently. Their investigation brings up problems that ought to be clarified, lest proportionality might paradoxically serve arbitrariness, although it was conceived to fight it.

3.6.3.3.2. Applicability

3.6.3.3.2.1. Relation between means and purpose

Proportionality is an applied normative postulate arising out of the norms and the distributive function of the Law as principles whose application depends on the juxtaposition of legal goods and the existence of a intersubjectively controllable means-purpose relation.[79] If there is not a properly structured means-purpose relation, then — as MAURER puts it — the exam of proportionality falls apart in the void for lacking points of reference.[80]

The exam of proportionality is applied every time there is a *concrete measure* aimed at achieving a *purpose*. In this case, one must analyze the chances of the measure leading to the realization of the purpose (exam of appropriateness), of the measure being the least restrictive to the rights involved among those that could have been used to achieve the purpose (exam of necessity) and of the public purpose being so valuable that it would justify such restriction (exam of proportionality in a narrow sense).

Without a relation of means and purpose, the postulate of proportionality cannot be examined due to the lack of elements to scaffold it. In this sense, it is important to investigate the meaning of *purpose*: a purpose is an expected concrete (extralegal) result; a result that can be imagined even without legal norms and concepts, such as obtaining, accumulating or dissipating goods, achieving given states or meeting certain conditions, causing or hindering actions.[81]

As one can see, the applicability of the postulate of proportionality depends on a relation of causation between means and purpose. If it is so, its scaffolding force resides in the way one can appraise the effects of using the means and in how the purpose of the measure is justified. Means with undefined effects and purposes with unclear outlines certainly weaken the control of proportionality over acts of the government, if not impeding it altogether.

A purpose is a desired state of affairs. What principles set forth is exactly the duty to advance purposes. In order to scaffold the application of the postulate of proportionality, it is indispensable to set forth purposes gradually. A vague and unclear purpose hardly allows one to check whether it is gradually furthered by adopting a certain means. Moreover, the exams themselves change depending on the definition of purposes; a measure can be appropriate or not depending on how the purpose can be defined.

3.6.3.3.2.2. Internal and external purposes

Law has several sorts of purposes. Hence, one can distinguish internal and external purposes.

Internal purposes set forth a result to be achieved, which resides in the very person or situation being compared and analyzed.[82] Comparing two people due to their economic capacity shows a close relationship between the measure (economic capacity) and the aimed purpose (collecting taxes). The same relationship is present when one relates *fault* and *penalty* or *fee* and *retribution*: the punishment must fit the crime; the fee must fit the service. The key point is that internal purposes require some measures of assessment that relate with people or situations, and they must carry on a property relevant to a given treatment. Hence the reason one refers measures of justice or judgments: tax-paying capacity is a measure, since it is a criterion for fair taxation, as much as it is a purpose, since it sets forth something whose existence justifies the very accomplishment of equality. Tax-paying capacity does not bring forth fairness of taxation; and the *means* and the *purpose* get mixed because they can not be told apart accurately.[83] As a consequence, the equality exam from an internal purpose viewpoint and a measure of justice demand nothing more than an exam of correspondence.

External purposes set forth results that are not qualities or properties of the subjects thus reached; rather, they are goals assigned to the State which have a dimension beyond legality.[84] Thus, two different realities at a concrete level can be set apart: the relation between means and purpose is a relation between cause and effect.[85] External purposes are those that can be empirically dimensioned so that one can say that a given idea is the means to achieve a certain goal (causation).[86] Social and economic purposes can be qualified as external purposes, as administrative practicability, specific economical planning and environmental protection are. When there is a specific purpose to reach, the means can be understood as the cause of the realization of the purpose. In this case, the exam can take the control of appropriateness, necessity and proportionality in a narrow sense.

This is exactly the point where proportionality is to be separated from other postulates or hermeneutic principles. The postulate of proportionality is not to be mixed with *fair proportion*: whereas the latter requires a proportion of the goods that entangle on a given legal relation, regardless of the existence of a restriction arising from a measure used to reach an external purpose, the postulate of proportionality requires appropriateness, necessity and proportionality in a narrow sense of a measure intended as the means to reach an empirically controllable purpose. The postulate of proportionality does not equal the *counterweighing of goods*: the latter requires assigning a dimension of importance to values that juxtapose, without any provision regarding the way this weighing is to be done, whereas the postulate of proportionality has precise requirements concerning the kind of reasoning to be employed in the application. The postulate of proportionality does not equal that of *practical accordance*: the latter requires the maximum realization of juxtaposing values also without any reference to the way this optimization is implemented, whereas proportionality relates means and the purpose through a rational structure of application. The postulate of proportionality is not to be mixed up with the *prohibition of excess*: the latter prohibits the restriction of the minimum potency of principles even in the absence of an external purpose to accomplish, whereas *proportionality* requires a proportional relation of a means regarding a purpose. The postulate of proportionality does not equal *reasonableness*: the latter requires attention to the individual particularities of the subjects within the scope of the actual application of the Law, without any mention to a proportion of means and purposes.

3.6.3.3.3. Inherent exams to proportionality

3.6.3.3.3.1. Appropriateness

Appropriateness requires an empirical relation between means and purpose: the means must lead to the realization of the purpose. Understanding the relation of means and purpose demands answers to three fundamental questions: what does it mean to be an appropriate means to realize a purpose? How is the relation of appropriateness to be analyzed? What should the degree of control over governmental decisions be?

In order to answer the first question (what does it mean to be an appropriate means to realize a purpose?), one needs first to analyze the kinds of relations that exist between the several means available and the purpose to be promoted. This relation can be analyzed from three viewpoints: quantitative (intensity), qualitative (quality) and probability (certainty).[87]

In quantitative terms, a means can further the purpose less than another, just as much, or more. In qualitative terms, a means can advance the purpose worse than another, just as well, or better. And, in probability terms, a means can promote the purpose less certainly, just as certainly, or more certainly than another. That means that the comparison of means legislators and administrators have to make is not always at the same level (quantitative, qualitative or probability) as the comparison is between a weaker and a stronger means, between a worse or better means, or between a less certain or a more certain means to further the purpose. The choice of the Administration when purchasing vaccines to fight an epidemic may involve comparing one that eradicates all symptoms of the disease (quantitatively best), but who is not proven to be effective for most of the population (inferior in probability terms) and another vaccine that has proven to be effective in other occasions (best in probability terms) in spite of curing only the main predicaments of the disease (quantitatively inferior).

These observation lead to the next and equally important question: Are the Administration and the legislators supposed to choose the *most intense*, *best*, and *safest* means to accomplish a purpose or are they supposed to choose means that "simply" further the purposes? The Administration and the legislators ought to choose means that "simply" further the purposes. Several reasons lead to this conclusion.[88]

First of all, it is not always possible — or even plausible — to know which, among all equally appropriate means, is the most intense, best and safest in realizing the purpose. That depends on information and circumstances that are often not available to the Administration. Governing would not be feasible — neither would the satisfactory promotion of its purposes be — if it had to assess all possible and imaginable means to achieve a purpose in order to make each and every decision, however trifling it might be.

Secondly, the principle of separation of powers demands respect for the objective will of the Legislative and Executive. Freedom of Administration would be previously decreased if judges could say that the chosen means was not the most appropriate after measures had already been taken. A minimal freedom of choice is innate to the system of division of functions.

Thirdly, the requirement of rational interpretation and application of the norms compels the analysis of all circumstances of a concrete case. Immediately excluding means that are not the *most intense*, the *best* and the *safest* to achieve a goal impedes examination of other arguments that may justify the choice. These other arguments should not, therefore, be analyzed in the exam of appropriateness, but in the exam of proportionality in a narrow sense, as will be shown below.

So far, it is enough to acknowledge that the Executive and Legislative Powers ought to choose means that minimally advance the purpose, even if not the most intense, best, or safest.

In order to answer the second question (how is the relation of appropriateness to be analyzed?), it is necessary to identify under which aspects appropriateness can be analyzed. It can be analyzed in three dimensions: abstract/concrete; general/particular; previous/subsequent.

The first dimension (abstract/concrete) may require adopting a measure that is abstractly appropriate to advance the purpose. The measure will be appropriate if the purpose can be *possibly* realized by adopting it. Whether such purpose is actually realized is not the point. Conversely, the adoption of a concretely appropriate measure can be required. The measure will be appropriate only if the purpose is indeed realized in actuality.

The second dimension (general/particular) may require adopting a measure that is generally appropriate to advance the purpose. The measure will be appropriate if the purpose is usually realized by adopting it. Even if a group is not reached or there are cases where the purpose is not accomplished with that measure, it will not be considered inappropriate just for that. Also, a measure may be required that is individually appropriate to further a purpose. The measure will be appropriate only if the purpose is realized in every particular case.

The third dimension (previous/subsequent) may require adopting a measure that is appropriate when it is adopted. The measure will be appropriate if the administrator assessed and designed the advancement of the purpose well at the time the measure was adopted. If the assessment of the administration is eventually shown to be wrong, by using information that arises later, that is beyond the point. Also, a measure may be required that is appropriate at the time of judgment. It will be found appropriate if the judge, at the time of the decision and afterwards, understands that the measure promotes the purpose. If the assessment of the administration is eventually shown to be wrong, with the information arising later, it ought to be annulled.

Because of all these, it is necessary to know what it means to adopt an appropriate measure. A definite answer is not feasible, given the many modes of operation of the government. Still, an answer can be proposed that stresses the heuristic value, i.e., an answer that works as a provisional hypothesis for a later reconstruction of normative content without ensuring any strictly deductive procedure of justification or decision regarding these contents, though.[89]

In this sense, one can say that, in the cases the government is working for a generality of cases — for instance, when it passes normative acts —, the measure will be appropriate if, in abstract and in general, it is a tool to further the purpose. However, in the case of merely individual acts — such as administrative acts —, the measure will be appropriate if, in concrete and individually, it works as the means to promote the purpose. In any of these two cases, appropriateness ought to be assessed at the time the government chooses the means and not later, when this choice is evaluated by a judge. This is because the quality of the assessment and design and, therefore, the quality of the work of the administration ought to be investigated in accordance with the circumstances at the time of the work. One must keep in mind that the exam of proportionality demands an analysis from the judge in which probability and induction decisions preponderate.[90]

These deliberations are extremely relevant from a practical point of view. One example to show it is the use in Tax Law of a mechanism through which the legislator, by law, replaces a taxpayer with another one that comes earlier on the supply chain and becomes liable for paying the due tax in advance. The use of this mechanism is apart from the traditional taxation scheme based on taxable events because of non-fiscal purposes, such as the simplification of tax collection and the smaller operation costs to audit it. It is structured on the assumption that the taxable event will eventually happen within certain dimensions. If the Legislative designed and assessed the measure well and correctly for cases in general, and estimated the "future taxable event" in average for each sector of the economy affected, individual occurrences that differ from the ones assumed do not affect the validity of the mechanism as such. In this case, the adopted measure is appropriate, because the required appropriateness, let us repeat, is not concrete, individual and subsequent, but abstract, general, and previous. The decisive matter, therefore, is the analysis of the legal mechanism in general and its abstract, general, and previous appropriateness for most of the cases, and not the exam of the taxable event in dimensions that differ from those assumed, or the investigation of whether tax costs with audition and collection of taxes actually decreased.

So far, it is enough to notice that the appropriateness of the means chosen by the government ought to be judged by considering the circumstances at the time of the choice and according to the way it contributes to the advancement of the purpose.

In order to answer the third question (what should the degree of control over governmental decisions be?), it is fundamental to analyze two levels of control: strong control and weak control.

In a model of strong control, any evidence that the means does not advence the realization of the ends is enough to assert the administrative act as invalid. In a weak model, only direct, obvious and justified evidence can lead to such assertion concerning the choice of means to reach an end. Well, which of these models is plausibly in accordance with the Brazilian legal order? The weak control model, for the reasons that follow.

Firstly, the principle of separation of powers requires minimal autonomy and independence to exercise legislative, administrative, and judicial functions. The legislator and administrator being granted minimum freedom, the judge is not entitled to choose the best means without a clear reason to find inappropriate the administration's choice of means to promote the end. The intersection between the duty to preserve the legislator's freedom and the duty to protect the citizen's fundamental rights reveals an abstract crossing where minimal freedom is spared for the legislator and for the administrator. Only a definite proof of inappropriateness will let one invalidate the choice of the legislator or administrator.[91]

These reflections reflect on the understanding that an exam of appropriateness only causes a declaration of nullity of the government's measure in the cases where means and ends are clearly incompatible. Otherwise, the option found by the organ with jurisdiction must prevail. Hence, one can understand why the Constitutional Court of the Federal Republic of Germany refers the controls of evidence (*Evidenzkontrole*) and justifiability (*Vertretbarkeitskontrole*). In order to preserve the functions of the Legislative and Executive, the Judiciary only decides to annul measures of other Powers if their inappropriateness is *evident* and not *justifiable* in any plausible way. Except for these cases, the choice of other Powers is to be sustained due to the principle of separation of powers. A merely bad estimate, by itself, does not make the chosen means invalid.

The precedents of the Supreme Court show, on one hand, the requirement of obviousness to void an inappropriate measure, and on the other hand the fact that an exam of appropriateness, or any other postulate for that matter, always involves the violation of some constitutional principle.

The Supreme Court examined the case of a statute that required realtors to prove conditions of ability to exercise their profession legally. The Court, however, opined that working as a realtor did not depend on said proof of ability. In other words, it declared that the means (certificate of ability) did not advance the ends (control of the profession). Consequently, this requirement violated the free exercise of any profession, employment or occupation.[92]

3.6.3.3.3.2. Necessity

The exam of necessity involves verifying the existence of means other than that initially chosen by the Legislative or Executive that may equally promote the ends without equally restricting the fundamental rights concerned. In this sense, the exam of necessity involves two stages of investigation: firstly, *the exam of equal appropriateness of the means*, to check whether alternative means equally advance the purpose; secondly, *the exam of the least restrictive means*, to examine whether the alternative means restrict collaterally affected fundamental rights to a smaller degree.

The exam of equal appropriateness of the means involves comparing the effects of using other means and the effects of using the one adopted by the Legislative or Executive. This exam is difficult because the means further the ends in several ways (qualitative, quantitative, probability). Not one equals another from every point of view. To some extent and from some point of view, means differ among themselves in furthering the ends. Some advance it more rapidly, others, more slowly; some spend less, and others, more; some are more certain, and others, more uncertain; some are simpler, and others, more complex; some are easier, and others, more difficult; and so on.[93] Besides that, the distinction of means will be obvious in some cases and obscure in others. Last, but not least: some means advance the purpose under exam more, as well as other related ends, whereas other means do not promote the purpose under exam as much, but promote others also set forth by the legal order more intensely.[94]

Given that, a question arises: are means to be compared *in every aspect* or only in *some aspects*? If only in *some aspects*, then which? The answer to this question ought to be sought with the same basis referred before, mostly the principle of separation of powers. If the Judiciary were allowed to annul the choice of some means because somehow, from some point of view, they do not advance the ends the same way others might possibly do, then no means would stand the control of necessity, since it is always possible to imagine, by induction and probability, other means to promote those ends better than the one chosen somehow and to some extent. In this sense, the choice of the authority with jurisdiction is to be respected, ruling the means out if clearly less appropriate than others. The principles of statutory legality and separation of powers demand it.

These previous thoughts make it clear that the identification of the least restrictive means ought to point to the lightest, most general means for the obvious cases. In the case of general norms, the necessary means is lightest or least harmful towards collateral fundamental rights in the average case. Exceptional cases may, with basis on the postulate of reasonableness, annul the general rules in general acts for neglecting the duty to grant minimal attention to the personal conditions of those affected. In the case of individual acts, where personal singularities and actual circumstances ought to be considered, the necessary means will be that of the concrete case.

The Supreme Court has applied the exam of necessity. The First Bench of the Court granted the habeas corpus requested by the presumed father of a minor born during his marriage, filed as a response to the lawsuit that aimed at acknowledging parenthood and rectifying records filed by a third party who alleged to be the child's biological father. The petitioner used the habeas corpus to avoid the embarrassment of being subject to a DNA test.

In this case, it was reasoned that the paternity investigation could be carried out without participation of the petitioner, since the plaintiff could take a DNA test himself.[95] The Court decided that the alternate means (testing the plaintiff for DNA) would be less restrictive than the one chosen by the district court judge (testing the defendant in the paternity lawsuit for DNA).

Likewise, the Supreme Court ruled as unconstitutional a statute that provided for the mandatory weighing of gas bottles in front of consumers, not only because it places an excessive burden on the companies, who would need scales on every truck, but also because consumer protection could be preserved in a different, less restrictive way.[96] In this case, the measure was declared unconstitutional because there were other measures less restrictive to the affected fundamental rights, such as inspections by sampling.

However, the exam of necessity is not simple at all. This is because, as mentioned before, comparing the degree of restriction of fundamental rights and the degree of furtherance of the mostly public purpose can be relatively complex. When two means that equally advance the purpose are compared, differing only in restrictiveness, it is easy to choose the least restrictive. There are problems, though, when the means are different not only regarding the restriction of fundamental rights, but also the degree of furtherance of the purpose. How can one choose between a means that little restricts a fundamental right, but little furthers the purpose, and another that strongly promotes the purpose but on the other hand restricts a fundamental right too much? Counterweighing the degree of restriction and the degree of furtherance is inevitable. Hence the necessity for the process of counterbalancing, as mentioned before, to involve an understanding of what is being weighed, the weighing itself and the reconstruction that follows weighing.

3.6.3.3.3.3. Proportionality in a narrow sense

The exam of proportionality in a narrow sense requires the comparison between the importance of realizing the end and the degree of restriction of the fundamental rights. The question to be asked is the following: does the degree of importance of promoting the end justify the degree of restriction affecting the fundamental rights? Or in other words: are the advantages of advancing the end proportional to the disadvantages of adopting the means? Does the value of promoting the end match the disregard for the consequent restriction?

It is, as one may see, a complex exam, because deciding what is an advantage and what is a disadvantage depends on an extremely subjective assessment. Usually, a means is adopted to meet a public purpose related to the interest of everyone (environmental protection, consumer protection), and adopting it collaterally affects fundamental rights of the citizen.

The Supreme Court found the measure disproportional in the previously mentioned opinion regarding the statute that provided for mandatory weighing of gas bottles in front of consumers. By reading the opinion, one can see that the degree of restrictions to the principles of free initiative and private property (excessive burden on companies, who would need scales on every truck, increase of cost that would be transferred to the price of bottles, and customers would have to walk to the trucks to observe the weighing) exceeded the importance of the promotion of the end (protection of consumers, who could be deceived into buying bottles without the content listed)[97].

3.6.3.3.4. Intensity of judiciary control of the other powers

One of the most relevant doubts concerning the application of the postulate of proportionality regards the intensity of Judiciary control over acts of the Executive and Legislative Powers. Besides the previous study of the weak control regarding adequacy, one must emphasize that the exercise of the prerogatives arising out of the democratic principle should be controlled by the Judiciary, mostly because it restricts fundamental rights. Instead of the non-controllability of such decisions (*Nichtjustitiabilität*), one should observe *to what extent* such competencies are exercised. In that sense, it is important to find criteria that broaden and restrict the substantive control the Judiciary may exercise.

On one hand, the scope of Judiciary control and the requirement of justification to a restriction of a fundamental right should be *greater*, the greater is: (1) the condition of the Judiciary to construe a safe judgment regarding the subject the Legislative regulated; (2) the evidence of mistake in the premise the Legislative has chosen to justify the restriction of a fundamental right; (3) the restriction to a constitutionally protected legal interest; (4) the importance of the constitutionally protected legal interest, measured by its founding nature or support function relative to other interests (e.g., life and equality) by its syntactical hierarchy in the constitutional order (e.g., fundamental principles).

In the presence of these factors, the Judiciary should exercise more control, notably when the Legislative premise is *obviously wrong*. This is so because the Judiciary has the duty of "assessing the assessment" of the Legislative (or Executive) relative to the chosen premise, since the Legislative will not realize the democratic principle to its maximum extent unless it chooses a concrete premise that *best promotes* the public goal that motivates its action or it has a justifying reason to reject the choice of a better premise. If the Legislative could have made a better assessment, without increasing expenses, its jurisdiction was not exercised according to the democratic principle that has to be maximized.

On the other hand, the scope of Judiciary control and the requirement of justification to a restriction of a fundamental right should be *smaller*, the more it is: (1) doubtful what the future effects of the act will be; (2) difficult and technical to deal with the subject; (3) open to the Legislative to consider the matter, according to the Constitution.

In the presence of these factors, the Judiciary should exercise less control, since it has greater difficulty making autonomous decisions. In any case – this is the key point – it will be the Judiciary's duty to decide whether the legislator has performed an objective and sustainable assessment of the factual and technical material available, and has exhausted sources of knowledge to forecast the effects of the rule to the safest extent, and has done such as the current stages of knowledge and experience direct.[98] If – but only if – all of these have been done, the decision of the Legislative is justifiable (*vertretbar*) and prevents the Judiciary from simply changing its assessment. It should be noted that the decision on the justification of the Legislative measure is the final result of the Judiciary control, and not a rigid position prior to such controlling act. Without Judiciary control, one cannot even affirm the justifiability of another Power's measure.

All of this leads to an understanding that constitutional control can be greater or smaller, but it will always exist; one must promptly reject the easy solution of denying the Judiciary any control of another power because of the separation of powers. The democratic principle will only be accomplished if the Legislative chooses concrete premises that lead to the realization of fundamental rights and governmental goals. The more restrict and important fundamental rights are in the constitutional order, the more their realization should be controlled. The theory of the non-controllability of the decisions of the Legislative, lacking of any elaborate support, is a monstrosity that violates the function of overseer of the Constitution assigned to the Supreme Court. It also violates the full realization of the democratic principle and fundamental rights as well as the realization of the principle of universal jurisdiction.

3.7. CONSEQUENCES OF THE LACK OF DIFFERENTIATION BETWEEN POSTULATES

By not differentiating proportionality from reasonableness from prohibition of excess, jurisprudence is oblivious of the fact that these postulates (metanorms of application of others in the case of conflicting experiences on the concrete and efficacy planes) work as parameters to relate different elements in distinct situations. The concrete exam performed when two principles collide on the basis of a relation of means and goals is not the same performed when a general rule and an exceptional case are incompatible. The justifications are different and – here is the main point – may lead to different results.

One example may clarify the point: enforcing a fine of 60% when a tax due is paid one day late. There are three exams that may be performed: checking if this general rule applies to the individual case (e.g. the delay occurred because of a duly proven accident with the employee who was on his way to the bank to make the payment), or whether there was a different means to realize the goal and the benefits are greater than the harms (30% might be enough to prevent late payments, and the bankruptcy of small business owners might be more harmful than assuring the punctuality of most), or whether the obligation violates the essential core of a fundamental right (an increase of 60% on the amount due, for a one-day delay, might attack the core of the right to property, regardless of the need or advantages of adopting the measure). These three exams are not identical in their elements and criteria. They can be given any name, but it cannot be said that the same balancing is performed in all of them. Hence, regardless of the word (proportionality, reasonableness, excess, arbitrariness), whether the same for all or one for each concrete reasoning, what matters is that there are different concrete exams that require different justification (because of the elements and criteria). To shuffle around these different concrete exams is to make the correct application of the Law impossible.

It is even worse to spend energy in sustaining that the discussion is merely about terminology. It may even be plausible, for those who do not pursue accuracy in the use of language and coherent clarity in justification, to use a single term for the three exams, or others for each of them. What is by no means acceptable is to use a single term or other terms interchangeably, thus ignoring the existence of three concrete exams that differ in their elements and parameters: an assessment of the relation between the degrees of promotion and restriction of colliding principles as a result of the adoption of a measure used with the expectation of promoting a goal whose realization is determined by one of the principles (such exam hereafter called "x"); an assessment of the relationship between a general rule and the individual case or between what is imposed and its consequence (reasoning hereafter called "y"); or an assessment of the relation between an imposing norm and the restriction of the core of a principle (exam hereafter called "z").

The problem is not to say that it is all a matter of choosing between the names "x", "y" and "z". The problem is to think that all exams can be encompassed by a single category "x", "y" or "z", when they actually involve different relationships and parameters, so much so that they allow different results: a norm can be applied in accordance with requirement "x" and still not be in accordance with "y" or "z", and so on and so forth. Moreover, a norm can be subject to control "x" although it is not subject to control "y". In sum, "x", "y" and "z" substantiate different exams.

Therefore, the problem is not to verify whether the use of different names implies different content exams. Rather, it is to verify whether the existence of different content exams requires the use of different terms: "x" for a multilateral exam that ultimately divides or apportions exterior legal assets; "y" for a unilateral exam of equity; and "z" for an exam of the limit of restrictions.

Indeed, the exam of reasonableness-equivalence investigates the relationship between two dimensions or between a measure and the criterion that determines it. The exam of proportionality investigates the relationship between the measure adopted, the goal to be realized and the degree of restriction to the fundamental rights in scope. The exam of prohibition of excess analyzes whether the essential core of a fundamental principle has been breached.

Given that, it is clear that the exams of reasonableness, proportionality and excessivity are concrete exams that differ from one another. It is also clear why there is so much confusion among them: the expressions "reasonableness", "proportionality" and "excessivity", when not used for the concrete exams they intend to represent, may refer to different concrete exams. In the case of the fine, the lack of equivalence between the amount and the gravity of the punishable conduct is unreasonable. However, such lack can be referred to as being "out of proportion", or one could say that the fine "exceeds" the amount that would be appropriate to punish the wrong. The same holds true for other cases.

Does that mean, then, that every discussion between "reasonableness", "proportionality" and "excessivity" is only a matter of consensus? No. Instead, it means that these expressions are ambiguous and ought to be defined, and deciding which of them will be used for which exam is secondary. What ought to be clear – and this is the central issue – is that there are three different concrete exams that ought not to be confused because they involve distinct elements related to different parameters. The problem is not whether to use either expression, but to confuse different concrete exams by using a single expression or several alternate expressions. In other words: the problem is not to use a single word for three phenomena, but not to realize there are three different phenomena to analyze.

Finally, it is important to note that in all of these exams there is a reasoning that is performed relative to the application of other norms of the legal order. The exam of reasonableness-equivalence analyzes the norm that establishes an intervention or action with the goal of identifying the equivalence between its dimension and the wrong it seeks to punish. The exam of proportionality investigates the norm that establishes the intervention or action to verify whether the principle that justifies its enactment will be promoted and the extent to which other principles will be restricted. This is the reason why this exam brings up the greater or lesser restriction to the fundamental principles. The exam of prohibition of excess analyzes the norm that establishes the intervention or action to prove whether any fundamental principle is being attacked in its core. This is the reason why it brings up the question of whether there is an excessive restriction of the fundamental principles.

That shows that these exams investigate *how* other norms ought to be applied, either by establishing criteria or by establishing measures. In any way, the requirements of reasonableness, proportionality and prohibition of excess flow onto other norms, though not to assign them meaning, but to rationally structure their application. There is always another norm behind the application of reasonableness, proportionality and excessivity. This is the reason why it is convenient to treat them as metanorms. And because they structure the application of other norms, with which they cannot be confused, it is convenient to refer to them by a different name. Therefore the use of the term "postulate" to indicate a norm that structures the application of others.

Postulates differ from the norms whose application they structure in several aspects: regarding level (postulates are on a metalevel or second level, and the norms under application are on an object level or first level), regarding the object (postulates indicate the structure of application of other norms and norms describe behaviors, if rules, or set forth the promotion of goals, if principles) and regarding the addressee (postulates are directed to judges and norms are directed to those who ought to abide by such norms).

These subtleties concerning the nature of the normative species being used and the control that is exercised contribute decisively to a greater effectivity of the constitutional principles, because the judge has better conditions to know what ought to be justified, what ought to be proven and which norms have their restriction of effectivity under analysis.

NOTES

1. EISLER, Rudolf. Kant-Lexikon. Hildesheim: Georg Olms Verlag, 1994. p. 427.
2. CANARIS, Claus-Wilhelm. *Systemdenken und Systembegriff in der Jurisprudenz*. Berlin: Duncker und Humblot, 1983. p. 16. See also: KERCHOVE, Michel van de. OST, François. *Le système juridique entre ordre et desordre*. Paris: PUF, 1988. p. 101.
3. ALEXY, Robert. Juristische Interpretation. *In: Recht, Vernunft, Diskurs*. Frankfurt am Main: Suhrkamp, 1995, p. 75 and on.

4. For example, as in: *STERN, Klaus. Das Staatsrecht der Bundesrepublik Deutschland.* Volume I: *Grundbegriffe und Grundlagen des Staatsrechts, Strukturprinzipien der Verfassung*, 2nd ed. Munich: Beck, 1984. p. 113 and on. HAEFLINGER, Arthur. *Die Hierarchie von Verfassungsnormen und ihre Funktion beim Schutz der Menschenrechte*, in: EuGRZ 1990, pp. 475–482. Disagreeing: HERZOG, Roman. *Hierarchie von Verfassungsnormen und ihre Funktion beim Schutz der Grundrechte*, in: EuGRZ 1990, pp. 483–486.
5. Concerning this matter, see: ALEXY, Robert. *Theorie der Grundrechte*. 2nd ed. Frankfurt am Main: Suhrkamp, 1994. pp. 94, 139, 140. BYDLINSKI, Franz. *Fundamentale Rechtsgrundsätze*. Vienna and New York: Springer, 1988. p. 125.
6. CARVALHO, Paulo de Barros. *Curso de Direito Tributário*. 7th ed. São Paulo: Saraiva, 1995. p. 138.
7. BOBBIO, Noberto. *Teoria dell'ordinamento giuridico*. Turin: Giappichelli, 1960. p. 46.
8. GUASTINI, Riccardo. *Le fonti del diritto e l'interpretazione*. Milan: Giuffrè, 1993. p. 37 and on. Idem. GUASTINI, Riccardo. *Teoria e dogmatica delle fonti*. Milan: Giuffrè, 1998. p. 121 and on.
9. CANARIS, Claus-Wilhelm. *Systemdenken und Systembegriff in der Jurisprudenz*. Berlin: Duncker und Humblot, 1983, p. 16 ("...in fact, it is mainly an axiological postulate!"); EISLER, Rudolf. Kant-Lexikon. Hidelsheim: Georg Olms Verlag, 1994. p. 427. GUASTINI, Riccardo. *Teoria e dogmatica delle fonti*. Milan: Giuffrè, 1998. p. 124, number 10: the author mentions a principle, but in the sense of a criterion. ALEXY, Robert. Juristische Interpretation. *In: Recht, Vernunft, Diskurs*. Frankfurt am Main: Suhrkamp, 1995. p. 75 and on: when analyzing hermeneutics as a structural theory of understanding, the author mentions postulates (e.g. reflection, coherence, completeness). KERCHOVE, Michel van de. OST, François. *Le système juridique entre ordre et desordre*. Paris: PUF, 1988. p. 101: authors refer to the systematization postulate as a permanent requirement to elaborate and apply the Law. PECZENIK, Aleksander. *Scientia Juris: Legal Doctrine as Knowledge of Law and as a Source of Law*. Dordrecht: Springer, 2005. p. 139: the author mentions the "postulate of the unity of law". Idem. Certainty or Coherence? *In: Festschrift for Aulis Aarnio*. Ed. Werner Krawietz and alli. Berlin: Duncker und Humblot, 2000. p. 168: the author mentions the "Postulate that the Law Should Be Coherent".
10. BRACKER, Susanne. *Kohärenz und juristische Interpretation*. Baden-Baden: Nomos, 2000. p. 169 and on.
11. MACCORMICK, Neil. *Rhetoric and The Rule of Law: A Theory of Legal Reasoning*. Oxford: Oxford, 2005. p. 192. Idem. *Legal Reasoning and Legal Theory*. Oxford: Oxford, 1978.p. 157.
12. MACCORMICK, Neil. *Rhetoric and The Rule of Law: A Theory of Legal Reasoning*. Oxford: Oxford, 2005. p. 190. Idem. Coherence in Legal Justification. *In: Theory of Legal Science*. Ed. Aleksander Peczenik et alli. Dordrecht: Reidel, 1984. p. 235 and on.
13. MACCORMICK, Neil. *Rhetoric and The Rule of Law: A Theory of Legal Reasoning*. Oxford: Oxford, 2005. p. 190.
14. GUSY, Christoph. *Parlamentarischer Gesetzgeber und Bundesverfassungsgericht*. Berlin: Duncker und Humblot, 1982. p. 191. In that respect, in Tax Law: LANG,

Joachim. Familienexistenzminimum im Steuer- und Kindergeldrecht. *StuW* (4):334, 1990. Important decision: BVerfGE 37, 217 (261).

15. PECZENIK, Aleksander. *On Law and Reason*. Dordrecht: Kluwer, 1989. p. 162. ALEXY, Robert. Juristische Begründung. *In: Rechtsdogmatik und praktische Vernunft*. Org. Okko Behrends et alli. Göttingen: Vandenhoeck u. Ruprecht, 1989. p. 98.
16. ALEXY, Robert. *Juristische Interpretation*. In: Recht, Vernunft, Diskurs. Frankfurt am Main: Suhrkamp, 1995, p. 86.
17. CANARIS, Claus-Wilhelm. *Systemdenken und Systembegriff in der Jurisprudenz*. Berlin: Duncker und Humblot, 1983. p. 13. BYDLINSKI, Franz. *System und Prinzipien des Privatrechts*. Vienna and New York: Springer, 1996. p. 3.
18. BYDLINSKI, Franz. *Fundamentale Rechtsgrundsätze*. Vienna and New York: Springer, 1988. pp. 126–127. MACCORMICK, Neil. *Legal Reasoning and Legal Theory*. Oxford: Oxford, 1978. p. 157. Idem. *Rhetoric and The Rule of Law: A Theory of Legal Reasoning*. Oxford: Oxford, 2005. p. 199.
19. Concerning this matter, see: STEGMÜLLER, Wolfgang. *Hauptströmungen der Gegenwartsphilosophie*. 7th ed. Volume I. p. 404.
20. VOGEL, Klaus. *Wordwide vs. source of taxation of income – A review and re-evaluation of arguments*. International Tax Review (Org.), Fred C. de Hosson, Offprint from Intertax 8-11/1988, p. 393. See also: CARRAZZA, Roque Antonio. *Curso de Direito Constitucional Tributário*. 11th ed. São Paulo: Malheiros, 1998. pp. 37–38.
21. BYDLINSKI, Franz. *System und Prinzipien des Privatrechts*. Vienna and New York: Springer, 1996. p. 16.
22. BYDLINSKI, Franz. *Fundamentale Rechtsgrundsätze*. Vienna and New York: Springer, 1988. pp. 40, 69 e 70.
23. GUASTINI, Riccardo. *Teoria e dogmatica delle fonti*. Milan: Giuffrè, 1998, p. 282. MACCORMICK, Neil. *Legal Reasoning and Legal Theory*. Oxford: Oxford, 1978. p. 157.
24. MOREIRA NETO, Diogo de Figueiredo. A ordem econômica na Constituição de 1988. *Revista de Direito Processual da Procuradoria Geral*, Rio de Janeiro (42):59–60, 1990.
25. PECZENIK, Aleksander. *On Law and Reason*. Dordrecht: Kluwer, 1989. p. 166.
26. PECZENIK, Aleksander. *On Law and Reason*. Dordrecht: Kluwer, 1989. p. 167. ALEXY, Robert. Juristische Begründung. *In: Rechtsdogmatik und praktische Vernunft*. Org. Okko Behrends et alli. Göttingen: Vandenhoeck and Ruprecht, 1989. p. 103. BRACKER, Susanne. *Kohärenz und juristische Interpretation*. Baden-Baden: Nomos, 2000. p. 107.
27. SANCHIS, Luis Prieto. Observaciones sobre las antinomías y el critério de ponderación. *In: Revista de Ciencias Sociales*. Facultad de Derecho y Ciencias Sociales, Universidad de Valparaiso, Chile, nº 45, 2000, p. 472.
28. ADIn (Writ of Declaration of Unconstitutionality) nº 855-2, Opinion by Justice Sepúlveda Pertence, DJU Oct 1st, 1993.
29. Habeas Corpus º 76060-SC, Opinion by Justice Sepúlveda Pertence. DJ May 15, 1998, p. 44.
30. ALEXY, Robert. *Theorie der Grundrechte*. 2nd ed. Frankfurt am Main: Suhrkamp, 1994. p. 100. About the subject, viewing ALEXY as clearly in favor of proportionality

as a rule, see: BOROWSKI, Martin. *Grundrechte als Prinzipien*. Baden-Baden: Nomos, 1998. p. 77. CLÉRICO, Laura. *Die Struktur der Verhältnismässigkeit*. Baden-Baden: Nomos, 2001. p. 21. SILVA, Virgílio Afonso da. O proporcional e o razoável. *Revista dos Tribunais*. v. 789. São Paulo: RT, 2002. p. 27.

31. Cf. BOROWSKI, Martin. *Grundrechte als Prinzipien*. Baden-Baden: Nomos, 1998. p. 91. SIECKMANN, Jan-Reinard. *Regelmodelle und Prinzipien-modelle des Rechtssystems*. Baden-Baden: Nomos, 1990. p. 84.
32. GUERRA FILHO, Willis S. *Teoria da Ciência Jurídica*. São Paulo: Saraiva, 2001. pp. 136 e 153.
33. TORRES, Ricardo Lobo. A legitimação dos Direitos Humanos e os Princípios da Ponderação e da Razoabilidade. *In: Legitimação dos Direitos Humanos*. TORRES, Ricardo Lobo, org. Rio de Janeiro: Renovar, 2002. p. 432.
34. MICHAEL, Lothar. *Der allgemeine Gleichheitssatz als Methodennorm komparativer Systeme*. Berlin: Duncker und Humblot, 1997. p. 42 e ss.
35. ADIn (Writ of Declaration of Unconstitutionality) nº855-2, Opinion by Justice Sepúlveda Pertence, DJU Oct 1st, 1993.
36. PECZENIK, Aleksander. The passion for reason. *In: The Law in Philosophical Perspectives*. Ed. Luc J. Wintgens. Dordrecht: Kluwer, 1999. p. 184.
37. STEINMETZ, Wilson Antônio. *Colisão de Direitos Fundamentais e o princípio da proporcionalidade*. Porto Alegre: Livraria do Advogado, 2001. p. 143.
38. SANTIAGO, José Mª. Rodríguez de. *La ponderación de bienes e interesses en el Derecho Administrativo*. Madrid: Marcial Pons, 2000. p. 111.
39. MARX, Michael. *Zur Definition des Begriffs »Rechtsgut«: Prolegomena einer materialen Verbrechenslehre*. Cologne: Carl Heymanns, 1971. p. 68.
40. ALEXY, Robert. Rechtsregeln und Rechtsprinzipien, *Archives Rechts und Sozialphilosophie*, Beiheft 25 (1985), p. 24.
41. CLÉRICO, Laura. *Die Struktur der Verhältnismäßigkeit*. Baden-Baden: Nomos, 2001. p. 165. SANTIAGO, José Mª. Rodríguez de. *La ponderación de bienes e interesses en el Derecho Administrativo*. Madrid: Marcial Pons, 2000. p. 117 and on.
42. HABERMAS, Jürgen. *Faktizität und Geltung*. Frankfurt am Main: Suhrkamp, 1992. p. 317.
43. ÁVILA, Humberto. Argumentação jurídica e a imunidade do livro eletrônico. Revista de Direito Tributário n. 79. São Paulo: Malheiros, 2001. Idem: *Materiell verfassungsrechtliche Beschränkungen der Besteuerungsgewalt in der brasilianischen Verfassung und im deutschen Grundgesetz*. Nomos: Baden-Baden, 2002. p. 375 and on.
44. DÜRIG, Günther. In: Munz/Dürig/Herzog/Scholz. *Grundgesetz Kommentar*. Article 3, Paragraph I, Margin Number 121 and 128.
45. TIPKE, Klaus. *Die Steuerrechtsordnung*. B I. Cologne: Otto Schmidt, 1993. p. 232 and 423.
46. Recurso Extraordinário Appeal n.º 18.331/SP, Opinion by Justice Orozimbo Nonato, DJ Oct. 21, 1951.
47. Representação nº 1.077-5/RJ, Opinion by Justice Moreira Alves, DJ Feb. 26, 1981.
48. Recurso Extraordinário Appeal nº 47.937/Guanabara, DJ Nov. 19, 1962.

49. ÁVILA, Humberto Bergmann. Estatuto do contribuinte: conteúdo e alcance. Revista da Associação Brasileira de Direito Tributário, (7):73–104, Belo Horizonte: Del Rey, 2001. Idem. *Materiell verfassungsrechtliche Beschränkungen der Besteuerungsgewalt in der brasilianischen Verfassung und im deutschen Grundgesetz*. Nomos: Baden-Baden, 2002. p. 75. Recent and precise: SILVA, Luis Virgílio Afonso da. O proporcional e o razoável. Revista dos Tribunais. RT: São Paulo, 2002. p. 27.
50. Concerning the matter, read, above all, this excellent article by BANDEIRA DE MELLO, Celso Antônio. *O conteúdo jurídico do princípio da igualdade*. 3. ed. São Paulo: Malheiros, 2001. Read also: MICHAEL, Lothar. *Der allgemeine Gleichheitssatz als Methodennorm komparativer Systeme*. Berlin: Duncker und Humblot, 1997. p. 42 e ss.
51. KIRCHHOF, Paul. *Die Verschiedenheit der Menschen und die Gleichheit vor dem Gesetz*. München: Siemens Stiftung, 1996. p. 8 e ss.
52. VOGEL/WALDHOFF. *Bonner Kommentar zum Grundgesetz*. 81st printing. 1997. p. 388. BIRK, Dieter. *Steuerrecht I, Allgemeines Steuerrecht*. 2nd ed. Munich: Beck, 1994. pp. 10–11. HUSTER, Stefan. *Rechte und Ziele: Zur Dogmatik des allgemeinen Gleichheitssatzes*. Berlin: Duncker und Humblot, 1993. pp. 149, 166–167, 210.
53. Concerning the multiplicity of meanings, see: SCACCIA, Gino. *Gli 'strumenti' della ragionevolezza nel giudizio costituzionale*. Milan: Giuffrè, 2000. Concerning the issue, read: ZAGREBELSKY, Gustavo. Su ter aspetti della ragionevolleza. *In: Il principio di ragionevolezza nella giurisprudenza della Corte Costituzionale*. Milan: Giuffrè, 1994. p. 179 and on. CERRI, Augusto. *Corso de Giustizia Costituzionale*. 2nd ed. Milan: Giuffrè, 1997. p. 233 and on.
54. SILVA, Virgílio Afonso da. O proporcional e o razoável. *Revista dos Tribunais*, v.798. São Paulo: RT, 2002. p. 34.
55. Habeas Corpus nº 71408-1, Second Bench, Opinion by Justice Marco Aurélio, DJ Oct. 29, 1999.
56. Recurso Extraordinário Appeal nº 192553-1, Second Bench, Opinion by Justice Marco Aurélio, DJ April 16, 1999.
57. Embargos de Declaração em Recurso Extraordinário nº 199066-0, Second Bench, Opinion by Justice Marco Aurélio, Aug. 1st, 1997.
58. Processo nº 13003.000021/99-14, Segunda Câmara do Segundo Conselho de Contribuintes. Sessão do dia 18.10.2000.
59. HAGE, Jaap. C. *Reasoning with Rules. An Essay on Legal Reasoning and Its Underlying Logic*. Dordrecht: Kluwer, 1997. p. 114.
60. ARISTOTELE. *Etica Nicomachea*. Transl. Marcello Zanata. Milan: Rizzoli, 1994. p. 381 (margin numbers 1137 to 19 and on).
61. ZANCANER, Weida. Razoabilidade e moralidade: princípios concretizadores do perfil constitucional do Estado Social e Democrático de Direito. *Revista Diálogo Jurídico*, Salvador CAJ – Centro de Atualização Jurídica, ano I, nº 9, dezembro, 2001, p. 4. Available at <http://www.direitopublico.com.br>.
62. ADIn (Writ of Declaration of Unconstitutionality), Preliminary Decision, Full Bench, Opinion by Justice Celso de Mello, DJ May 26, 1995.

63. ADIn (Writ of Declaration of Unconstitutionality) nº 2.667-DF, Writ of Prevention, Opinion by Justice Celso de Mello, June 19, 2002.
64. ADIn (Writ of Declaration of Unconstitutionality) nº 247-RJ, Opinion by Justice Ilmar Galvão, June 17, 2002.
65. MOREIRA NETO, Diogo de Figueiredo. Moralidade administrativa: do conceito à efetivação. *RDA* (190):13, Rio de Janeiro: Renovar, 1992.
66. SCACCIA, Gino. *Gli 'strumenti' della ragionevolezza nel giudizio costituzionale.* Milan: Giuffrè, 2000. p. 247.
67. ZANCANER, Weida. Razoabilidade e moralidade: princípios concretizadores do perfil constitucional do Estado Social e Democrático de Direito. *Revista Diálogo Jurídico*, Salvador CAJ – Centro de Atualização Jurídica, ano I, nº 9, dezembro, 2001, p. 4. Available at <http://www.direitopublico.com.br>.
68. ADIn (Writ of Declaration of Unconstitutionality) nº 1.753-2, Full Bench, Opinion by Justice Sepúlveda Pertence, DJ June 12, 1998.
69. ADIn (Writ of Declaration of Unconstitutionality), Preliminary Decision, Full Bench, Opinion by Justice Sepúlveda Pertence, DJ Nov 22, 1991.
70. ADIn (Writ of Declaration of Unconstitutionality) nº 1.813-5, Full Bench, Opinion by Justice Marco Aurélio, DJ June 06, 1998.
71. Representação nº 1077, Revista Trimestral de Jurisprudência do Supremo Tribunal Federal 112/34-67.
72. Habeas Corpus nº 77003, Relator Ministro Marco Aurélio, DJ 11.09.98.
73. ÁVILA, Humberto. A distinção entre princípios e regras e a redefinição do dever de proporcionalidade. *RDA* (215):151–179, Rio de Janeiro: Renovar, jan./mar. 1999.
74. ÁVILA, Humberto Bergmann. *Materiell verfassungsrechtliche Beschränkungen der Besteuerungsgewalt in der brasilianischen Verfassung und im deutschen Grundgesetz.* Baden-Baden: Nomos, 2002. p. 71.
75. MENDES, Gilmar Ferreira. O princípio da proporcionalidade na jurisprudência do Supremo Tribunal Federal. *Direitos fundamentais e controle de constitucionalidade.* São Paulo: Celso Bastos Editor, 1998. p. 67 and on.
76. BARROSO, Luis Roberto. *Interpretação e aplicação da Constituição.* 4th ed. Rio de Janeiro: Renovar, 2001. p. 224 and on. BANDEIRA DE MELLO, Celso Antônio. *Curso de Direito Administrativo.* 13th ed. São Paulo: Malheiros, 2001. CLÉRICO, Laura. *Die Struktur der Verhältnismäßigkeit.* Baden-Baden: Nomos, 2001. p. 223 and on.
77. SILVA, Virgílio Afonso da. O proporcional e o razoável. *Revista dos Tribunais*, v. 798. São Paulo: RT, 2002. p. 28 and on.
78. Concerning the matter, read: ÁVILA, Humberto. A distinção entre princípios e regras e a redefinição do dever de proporcionalidade. *RDA* (215):151–179, Rio de Janeiro: Renovar, jan./mar. 1999.
79. JAKOBS, Michael Ch. *Der Grundsatz der Verhältnismäßigkeit.* Cologne: Carl Heymanns, 1985. p. 96.
80. MAURER, Hartmut. *Staatsrecht.* Munich: Beck, 1999. p. 234–235.
81. VOGEL, Klaus/WALDHOFF, Christian. *Grundlagen des Finanzverfassungsrechts: Sonderausgabe des Bonner Kommentars zum Grundgesetz (Vorbemerkungen zu Art. 104a bis 115 GG).* Heidelberg: Müller, 1999. margin number 480, p. 310.

82. HUSTER, Stefan. *Rechte und Ziele: Zur Dogmatik des allgemeinen Gleichheitssatzes.* Berlin: Duncker und Humblot, 1993. p. 166–167.
83. HUSTER, Stefan. *Rechte und Ziele: Zur Dogmatik des allgemeinen Gleichheitssatzes.* Berlin: Duncker und Humblot, 1993. p. 210, 149.
84. VOGEL, Klaus/WALDHOFF, Christian. *Grundlagen des Finanzverfassungsrechts: Sonderausgabe des Bonner Kommentars zum Grundgesetz (Vorbemerkungen zu Art. 104a bis 115 GG).* Heidelberg: Müller, 1999. margin number 480, p. 310.
85. HUSTER, Stefan. *Rechte und Ziele: Zur Dogmatik des allgemeinen Gleichheitssatzes.* Berlin: Duncker und Humblot, 1993. p. 148, 150.
86. HIRSCHBERG, Lothar. *Der Grundsatz der Verhältnismäßigkeit.* Göttingen: Otta Schwartz, 1981. p. 43.
87. WEINBERGER, Ota. *Rechtslogik.* 2nd ed. Berlin: Duncker und Humblot, 1989. p. 287. Concerning proportionality, read, above all, the brilliant work by CLÉRICO, Laura. *Die Struktur der Verhältnismäßigkeit.* Baden-Baden: Nomos, 2001. p. 26 and on.
88. Cf. CLÉRICO, Laura. *Die Struktur der Verhältnismäßigkeit.* Baden-Baden: Nomos, 2001. p. 39.
89. SCHEPERS, H. Heuristik. In: *Historisches Wörterbuch der Philosophie.* V. 3. Darmstadt: Wissenschaftliche Buchgesellschaft, 1974. p. 1119.
90. SCACCIA, Gino. *Gli 'strumenti' della ragionevolezza nel giudizio costituzionale.* Milan: Giuffrè, 2000. p. 20.
91. SCACCIA, Gino. *Gli 'strumenti' della ragionevolezza nel giudizio costituzionale.* Milan: Giuffrè, 2000. p. 238.
92. Representação nº 930-DF, Full Bench, Opinion by Justice Cordeiro Guerra, DJ Sept. 2nd, 1977.
93. WRIGHT, Georg von. *Rationalität: Mittel und Zwecke.* In: Normen, Werte und Handlungen. Frankfurt am Main: Suhrkamp, 1994. p. 126.
94. CLÉRICO, Laura. *Die Struktur der Verhältnismäßigkeit.* Baden-Baden: Nomos, 2001. p. 85.
95. Habeas Corpus nº 76060-SC, First Bench, Opinion by Justice Sepúlveda Pertence, DJ May 15, 1998.
96. ADIn (Writ of Declaration of Unconstitutionality) nº 855-2, Opinion by Justice Octávio Galloti, DJ Oct. 1st, 1993.
97. ADIn (Writ of Declaration of Unconstitutionality) nº 855-2, Opinion by Justice Octávio Galloti, DJ Oct. 1st, 1993.
98. RAU, Christian. *Selbst entwickelte Grenzen in der Rechtsprechung des United States Supreme Court und des Bundesverfassungsgerichts.* Berlin: Duncker und Humblot, 1996. pp. 192 and on. RAABE, Marius. Grundrechtsschutz und gesetzgeberischer Einschätzungsspielraum – Eins Konstruktiosvorschlag – *In: Allgemeinheit der Grundrechte und Vielfalt der Gesellschaft.* Org. Christoph Grabenwarter. Stuttgart: Boorberg, 1994. pp. 94 and on.

CHAPTER 4

CONCLUSIONS

1. The distinction between normative species, concerning its possible use in the application process, may be developed from their up-front meaning. Thus, the preliminary meaning of provisions can take a *dimension* that is immediately behavioral (rule), finalistic (principle) and/or methodical (postulate).
2. Rules are immediate descriptive norms, primarily past regarding, and expect to be decisive and broad, whose application requires an assessment of correspondence, always centered on the end that supports it and on the principles that are axiologically overlying to it, between the conceptual construction of the normative description and the conceptual construction of facts.
3. Principles are immediate finalistic norms, primarily future regarding, and expect to be complementary and partial, whose application requires an assessment of the correlation between the state of affairs to be promoted and the effects of the conduct considered necessary to such promotion.
4. Rules can be distinguished from principles regarding the way they describe a behavior. Rules are immediately descriptive norms, as they set forth obligations, permissions and prohibitions by describing the conduct to be followed. Principles are immediately finalistic norms, as they set forth a state of affairs whose gradual advancement depends on the effects of the adoption of behaviors necessary to it. Principle are norms whose up-front quality is exactly to determine the realization of a legally relevant purpose, whereas the up-front characteristic of rules is to establish a behavior.
5. Rules can be distinguished from principles regarding the justification they require. The interpretation and application of rules require an assessment of the matching between the conceptual construction of facts and the conceptual construction of the norm and the finality supporting it, whereas the interpretation and application of principles require an assessment of the correlation between the state of affairs set as a purpose and the effects of the conduct considered necessary.
6. Rules can be distinguished from principles regarding the way they contribute to a decision. Principles are primarily complementary and partially preliminary norms, for although they cover only part of the aspects relevant to make a decision, they do not expect to generate a

specific solution, but rather to contribute beside other reasons to make a decision. On the other hand, rules are preliminarily decisive and involving norms, for although they expect to cover all aspects relevant to make a decision, they expect to generate a specific solution for the conflict of reasons.

7. Normative postulates are immediately methodical norms that scaffold the interpretation and application of principles and rules by the more or less specific requirement of relations between elements according to criteria.
8. Some postulates are applied without presupposing the existence of specific criteria and elements: counterbalancing assets is a method aimed at assigning weights to elements that intertwine without reference to material points of view that guide this balancing; the practical accordance requires the maximum realization of juxtaposing values; the prohibition of excess prohibits the application of a rule or principle to restrict a fundamental right to an extent such that it loses all its efficacy.
9. The applicability of other postulates depends on certain conditions. The postulate of equality scaffolds the application of the law when there is a relation between two subjects due to elements (criterion of differentiation and purpose of distinction) and to the relation between them (congruence of the criterion regarding the purpose).
10. The postulate of reasonableness is applied firstly as a guideline that requires general norms to relate with individualities in actual cases, either by showing under which perspective the norm is to be applied or by showing when the individual case is so specific it does not fit the general norm. Secondly, as a guideline that requires a connection of legal norms with the world they refer to, either by claiming for an empirical and appropriate support for any legal act or by requiring a congruent relation between the adopted measure and the end it expects to reach. Thirdly, as a guideline that demands a relation of equivalence between two dimensions of magnitude.
11. The postulate of proportionality is applicable to the cases where there is a relation of causation between a means and an actually perceptible end. The requirement of realization of several ends, all constitutionally legitimate, causes the adoption of measures that are appropriate, necessary and proportional in a narrow sense.
12. A means is appropriate when it minimally advances the end. In the case of general legal acts, appropriateness is to be analyzed from an abstract, general, previous point of view. In the case of individual legal acts, appropriateness is to be analyzed at a concrete, individual,

previous level. Control of appropriateness ought to be limited, due to the principle of separation of powers, to annulling means that are obviously inappropriate.

13. A means is necessary when there are no alternate means that may equally promote the end without restricting affected fundamental rights to the same degree. Control of necessity ought to be limited, due to the principle of separation of powers, to annulling the chosen means when there is an alternate means that, from aspects considered fundamental, equally promote the ends with fewer restrictions.
14. A means is proportional when the value of furthering the end is not proportional to the disregard for the restriction to fundamental rights. In order to analyze it, necessary to compare the degree of furtherance of the end with the degree of restriction to the fundamental rights. The means will be disproportional if the importance of the end does not justify the degree of restriction to fundamental rights.

REFERENCES

AARNIO, Aulis. *Reason and Authority. A Treatise on the Dynamic Paradigm of Legal Dogmatics*. Aldershot: Ashgate, 1997.

Idem. *Denkweisen der Rechtswissenschaft*. Vienna: Springer, 1979.

ALEXANDER, Larry and SHERWIN, Emily. *The Rules of Rules – Morality, Rules and the Dilemmas of Law*. Durham and London: Duke University Press, 2001.

ALEXY, Robert. Zum Begriff des Rechtsprinzips. In: Argumentation und Hermeneutik in der Jurisprudenz, *Rechtstheorie*, Beiheft 1, Berlin: Dunckler und Humblot, 1979.

Idem. My Philosophy of Law: The Institutionalism of Reason. *In: The Law In Philosophical Perspectives*. Ed. Luc. Wintgens. Dordrecht: Kluwer, 1999.

Idem. On the structure of legal principles. *Ratio Juris* (13):300. Oxford: Blackwell, 2000.

Idem. Rechtsregeln und Rechtsprinzipien. *Archives Rechts und Sozialphilosophie*, Beiheft 25 (1985).

Idem. *Theorie der juristischen Argumentation*. 2nd ed. Frankfurt: Suhrkamp, 1991.

Idem. *Theorie der Grundrechte*. 2nd ed. Frankfurt am Main: Suhrkamp, 1994.

Idem. *Rechtssystem und praktische Vernunft*. In: Recht, Vernunft, Diskurs. Frankfurt am Main: Suhrkamp, 1995.

Item. Juristische Begründung. In: *Rechtsdogmatik und praktische Vernunft*. Org. Okko Behrends et alli. Göttingen: Vandenhoeck und Ruprecht, 1989.

Idem. Juristische Interpretation. In: Recht, Vernunft, Diskurs. Frankfurt am Main: Suhrkamp, 1995.

ARISTOTELE. *Etica Nicomachea*. Transl. Marcello Zanata. Milan: Rizzoli, 1994.

ÁVILA, Humberto Bergmann. A distinção entre princípios e regras e a redefinição do dever de proporcionalidade. *Revista de Direito Administrativo* (215):151–179, Rio de Janeiro: Renovar, jan./mar. 1999.

Idem. Repensando o princípio da supremacia do interesse público sobre o particular. *Revista Trimestral de Direito Público* (24):159–180, São Paulo: Malheiros, 1999.

Idem. Estatuto do Contribuinte: conteúdo e alcance. *Revista da Associação Brasileira de Direito Tributário* (07):73–104, Belo Horizonte: Del Rey, set/dez. 2000.

Idem. Argumentação jurídica e a imunidade do livro eletrônico. Revista de Direito Tributário n° 79. São Paulo: Malheiros, 2001.

Idem. *Materiell verfassungsrechtliche Beschränkungen der Besteuerungsgewalt in der brasilianischen Verfassung und im deutschen Grundgesetz*. Baden-Baden: Nomos, 2002.

Idem. Benefícios fiscais inválidos e a legítima expectativa dos contribuintes. *Revista Tributária* (42):100–114, São Paulo: Revista dos Tribunais, 2002.

Idem. *Sistema Constitucional Tributário*. São Paulo: Saraiva, 2004.

BANDEIRA DE MELLO, Celso Antônio. 3rd ed. *O conteúdo jurídico do princípio da igualdade*. São Paulo: Malheiros, 2001.

Idem. *Curso de Direito Administrativo*. 12th ed. 2nd printing. São Paulo: Malheiros, 2000.

Idem. *Curso de Direito Administrativo*. 13th ed. São Paulo: Malheiros, 2001.

BARCELLOS, Ana Paula. Some normative parameters for constitutional weighing. In: *A nova interpretação constitucional*. Org. Luis Roberto Barroso. Rio de Janeiro: Renovar, 2003.

BARROSO, Luis Roberto. *Interpretação e aplicação da Constituição.* 4th ed. Rio de Janeiro: Renovar, 2001.

BELTRÁN, Jordi Ferrer. *Las normas de competência.* Madrid: Boletín Oficial del Estado, 2000.

BIRK, Dieter. *Steuerrecht I, Allgemeines Steuerrecht.* 2nd ed. Munich: Beck, 1994.

BOROWSKI, Martin. *Grundrechte als Prinzipien.* Baden-Baden: Nomos, 1998.

BOBBIO, Noberto. *Teoria dell'ordinamento giuridico.* Turin: Giappichelli, 1960.

BRACKER, Susanne. *Kohärenz und juristische Interpretation.* Baden-Baden: Nomos, 2000.

BYDLINSKI, Franz. *Fundamentale Rechtsgrundsätze.* Vienna and New York: Springer, 1988.

Idem. *System und Prinzipien des Privatrechts.* Vienna and New York: Springer, 1996.

CANARIS, Claus-Wilhelm. *Systemdenken und Systembegriff in der Jurisprudenz.* Berlin: Duncker und Humblot, 1983.

Idem. *Die Feststellung von Lücken im Gesetz.* Berlin: Duncker und Humblot, 1982.

Idem. Theorienrezeption und Theorienstruktur. In: *Wege zum japanischen Recht. Festschrift für Zentaro Kitagawa.* Org. Hans G. Leser. Berlin: Duncker und Humblot, 1992.

Idem. Funkiton, Struktur und Falsifikation juristischer Theorien. *Juristen Zeitung*, nr. 8, p. 377–391, 1993.

CANOTILHO, J. J. Gomes. *Direito Constitucional e Teoria da Constituição.* 3rd ed. Coimbra: Almedina, 1999.

CERRI, Augusto. *Corso de Giustizia Costituzionale.* 2nd ed. Milan: Giuffrè, 1997.

CARRAZZA, Roque Antonio. *Curso de Direito Constitucional Tributário.* 11th ed. São Paulo: Malheiros, 1998.

CARVALHO, Paulo de Barros. *Curso de Direito Tributário.* 7th ed. São Paulo: Saraiva, 1995.

Idem. *Curso de Direito Tributário.* 14th ed. São Paulo: Malheiros, 2002.

Idem. *Direito Tributário: Fundamentos Jurídicos da Incidência.* São Paulo: Saraiva, 1998.

CLÉRICO, Laura. *Die Struktur der Verhältnismässigkeit.* Baden-Baden: Nomos, 2001.

DERZI, Misabel de Abreu Machado. Notas a BALEEIRO, Aliomar. *Limitações constitucionais ao Poder de Tributar.* 7th ed. Rio de Janeiro: Forense, 1997.

DÜRIG Günther. In: Munz/Dürig/Herzog/Scholz. *Grundgesetz Kommentar.* Article 3, Paragraph I, margin numbers 121 and 128. Munich: Beck, 1997.

DWORKIN, Ronald. The Model of Rules, *University of Chicago Law Review* 35 (1967).

Idem. Is law a system of rules? In: *The Philosophy of Law*, ed. by R. M. Dworkin. Oxford: Oxford University Press, 1977.

Idem. *Taking Rights Seriously.* 6th printing London: Duckworth, 1991.

ECKHOFF, Torstein. Legal Principles. In: *Prescriptive Formality and Normative Rationality in Modern Legal Systems.* Festschrift for Robert S. Summers. Berlin: Duncker und Humblot, 1994.

EISLER, Rudolf. Kant-Lexikon. Hidelsheim: Georg Olms Verlag, 1994.

ESSER, Josef. *Grundsatz und Norm in der richterlichen Fortbildung des Privatrechts.* 4th printing. Tübingen: Mohr Siebeck, 1990.

FERRAZ Jr. Tércio. *Função social da dogmática jurídica.* São Paulo: Max Limonad, 1997.

Idem. *Introdução ao estudo do Direito.* (*Introduction to Jurisprudence*) 3rd ed. São Paulo: Atlas, 2001.

FIGUEROA, Alfonso García. *Principios y positivismo jurídico.* Madrid: Centro de Estudios Políticos y Constitucionales, 1998.

GOTTLIEB, Stephen E. The Paradox of Balancing Significant Interests. *Hastings Law Journal.* v. 45, n. 4, April 1994.

GRAU, Eros Roberto. *Interpretação/Aplicação do Direito*. São Paulo: Malheiros, 2002.
GRECO, Marco Aurélio. *Contribuições (uma figura "sui generis")*. São Paulo: Dialética, 2000.
GUASTINI, Riccardo. *Teoria e dogmatica delle fonti*. Milan: Giuffrè, 1998.
Idem. *Dalle fonti alle norme*. Turin: Giappichelli, 1992.
Idem. Le fonti del diritto e l'interpretazione. Milan: Giuffrè, 1993.
Idem. Interprétation et description de normes. *In: Interpretation et Droit*. Org. Paul Amselek. Brussels: Bruylant, 1995.
Idem. *Distinguendo: studi dei teoria e metateoria del diritto*. Turin: Giappichelli, 1996.
Idem. *Il giudice e la legge*. Turin: Giappichelli, 1995.
GUERRA FILHO, Willis S. *Teoria da Ciência Jurídica*. São Paulo: Saraiva, 2001.
GÜNTHER, Klaus. *Der Sinn für Angemessenheit. Anwendungsdiskurse in Moral und Recht*. Frankfurt am Main: Suhrkamp, 1988.
GUSY, Christoph. *Parlamentarischer Gesetzgeber und Bundesverfassungsgericht*. Berlin: Duncker und Humblot, 1982.
HABERMAS, Jürgen. *Faktizität und Geltung*. Frankfurt am Main: Suhrkamp, 1992.
Idem. Wahrheitstheorien. In: *Vorstudien und Ergänzungen zur Theorie des kommunikativen Handels*. Frankfurt am Main: Suhrkamp, 1995.
HAGE, Jaap. C. *Reasoning with Rules. An Essay on Legal Reasoning and Its Underlying Logic*. Dordrecht: Kluwer, 1997.
HAEFLINGER, Arthur. *Die Hierarchie von Verfassungsnormen und ihre Funktion beim Schutz der Menschenrechte*, in: EuGRZ 1990, pp. 475–482.
HERZOG, Roman. *Hierarchie von Verfassungsnormen und ihre Funktion beim Schutz der Grundrechte*, in: EuGRZ 1990, pp. 483–486.
HERBERT, Manfred. *Rechtstheorie als Sprachkritik. Zum Einfluß Wittgensteins auf die Rechtstheorie*. Baden-Baden: Nomos, 1995.
HIRSCHBERG, Lothar. *Der Grundsatz der Verhältnismäßigkeit*. Göttingen: Otta Schwartz, 1981.
HUSTER, Stefan. *Rechte und Ziele: Zur Dogmatik des allgemeinen Gleichheitssatzes*. Berlin: Duncker und Humblot, 1993.
IVAINER, Thédore. *L'Interprétation des faits en droit*. Paris: LGDJ, 1988.
JAKOBS, Michael Ch. *Der Grundsatz der Verhältnismäßigkeit*. Cologne: Carl Heymanns, 1985.
JESTAEDT, Matthias. *Grundrechtsentfaltung im Gesetz*. Tübingen: Siebeck, 1999.
KAUFMANN, Arthur. *Analogie und 'Natur der Sache'*. 2nd ed. Heidelberg: Muller, 1982.
Idem. Die ipsa res iusta. In: *Beiträge zur Juristischen Hermeneutik*. 2nd ed. Cologne: Carl Heymanns, 1993.
KERCHOVE, Michel van de. OST, François. *Le système juridique entre ordre et desordre*. Paris: PUF, 1988.
KIRCHHOF, Paul. *Die Verschiedenheit der Menschen und die Gleichheit vor dem Gesetz*. Munich: Siemens Stiftung, 1996.
LANG, Joachim. Familienexistenzminimum im Steuer- und Kindergeldrecht. *StuW* (4):334, 1990.
LARENZ, Karl. *Richtiges Recht*. Munich: Beck, 1979.
Idem. *Methodenlehre der Rechtswissenschaft*. 6th ed. Munich: Beck, 1991.
LESSA, Pedro. *In: Biblioteca Internacional de Obras Célebres*. Volume XI. Lisbon: Sociedade Internacional, [19–]
MacCORMICK, Neil. *Legal Reasoning and Legal Theory*. Oxford: Oxford, 1978.

Idem. Coherence in Legal Justification. In: *Theory of Legal Science*. Ed. Aleksander Peczenik et alli. Dordrecht: Reidel, 1984. pp. 235–251.

Idem. Argumentation and Interpretation in Law. Ratio Juris v. 6. nº 1, p. 17. London: Blackwell, 1993.

Idem. *Rhetoric and The Rule of Law: A Theory of Legal Reasoning*. Oxford: Oxford, 2005.

MARX, Michael. *Zur Definition des Begriffs »Rechtsgut«: Prolegomena einer materialen Verbrechenslehre*. Cologne: Carl Heymanns, 1971.

MAURER, Hartmut. *Staatsrecht*. Munich: Beck, 1999.

MENDES, Gilmar Ferreira. O princípio da proporcionalidade na jurisprudência do Supremo Tribunal Federal. *Direitos fundamentais e controle de constitucionalidade*. São Paulo: Celso Bastos Editor, 1998.

MENDONÇA, Maria Luiza Vianna Pessoa de. *O princípio constitucional da irretroatividade da lei*. Belo Horizonte: Del Rey, 1996.

MICHAEL, Lothar. *Der allgemeine Gleichheitssatz als Methodennorm komparativer Systeme*. Berlin: Duncker und Humblot, 1997.

MODESTO, Paulo. Controle jurídico do comportamento ético da administração pública no Brasil. *RDA* (209):77, Rio de Janeiro: Renovar, 1997.

MONTAIGNE, Michel. Essais. Book III. Chapter XIII. In: Ouvres complètes. Paris: Éditions Gallimard, 1962.

MOREIRA NETO, Diogo de Figueiredo. Moralidade administrativa: do conceito à efetivação. *RDA* (190):13, Rio de Janeiro: Renovar, 1992.

Idem. A ordem econômica na Constituição de 1988. *Revista de Direito Processual da Procuradoria Geral*, Rio de Janeiro (42):59–60, 1990.

MÜLLER, Friedrich. Warum Rechtslinguistik? Gemeinsame Probleme von Sprachwissenschaft und Rechtstheorie. In: ERBGUTH, Wilfried; MÜLLER, Friedrich; Neumann, Volker (Orgs.). *Rechtstheorie und Rechtsdogmatik im Austausch. Gedächtnisschrift für Bernd Jeand'Heur*. Berlin: Duncker und Humblot, 1999.

PECZENIK, Aleksander. *On law and Reason*. Dordrecht: Kluwer, 1989.

Idem. The passion for reason. In: *The Law in Philosophical Perspectives*. Ed. Luc J. Wintgens. Dordrecht: Kluwer, 1999. p. 183.

Idem. Certainty or Coherence? In: *Festschrift for Aulis Aarnio*. Ed. Werner Krawietz and alli. Berlin: Duncker und Humblot, 2000. pp. 157–171.

Idem. *Scientia Juris: Legal Doctrine as Knowledge of Law and as a Source of Law*. Springer: Dordrecht, 2005.

PENSKY, Ulrich. Rechtsgrunsätze und Rechtsregeln. In: *Juristen Zeitung*, 3 (1989).

PESTANA, Márcio. *O princípio da imunidade tributária*. São Paulo: Revista dos Tribunais, 2001.

PILDES, Richard H. Avoiding Balancing: The Role of Exclusionary Reasons in Constitutional Law. *Hastings Law Journal*. v. 45, n. 4, April 1994.

RAABE, Marius. Grundrechtsschutz und gesetzgeberischer Einschätzungsspielraum - Eins Konstruktiosvorschlag. In: *Allgemeinheit der Grundrechte und Vielfalt der Gesellschaft*. Org. Christoph Grabenwarter. Stuttgart: Boorberg, 1994.

RAU, Christian. Selbst entwickelte Grenzen in der Rechtsprechung des United States Supreme Court und des Bundesverfassungsgerichts. Berlin: Duncker und Humblot, 1996.

RAZ, Joseph. *The Authority of Law – Essays on Law and Morality*. Oxford: Clarendon Press, 2002.

REALE, Miguel. *Cinco temas do culturalismo*. São Paulo: Saraiva, 2000.

Idem. *Lições preliminares de Direito.* (*First lessons on Law*) 23rd ed. São Paulo: Saraiva, 1996.

ROTHENBURG, Walter Claudius. *Princípios constitucionais.* Porto Alegre: Fabris, 1999.

SANCHIS, Luis Prieto. Observaciones sobre las antinomías y el critério de ponderación. In: *Revista de Ciencias Sociales.* Facultad de Derecho y Ciencias Sociales, Universidad de Valparaiso, Chile, nº 45, 2000.

SANTIAGO, José Mª. Rodríguez de. *La ponderación de bienes e interesses en el Derecho Administrativo.* Madrid: Marcial Pons, 2000.

SCACCIA, Gino. *Gli 'strumenti' della ragionevolezza nel giudizio costituzionale.* Milan: Giuffrè, 2000.

SCHAUER, Frederick. *Playing by the rules. A philosophical Examination of Rule-Based Decision-Making in Law and in Life.* Oxford: Clarendon, 1991.

Idem. Rules and The Rule of Law. *Harvard Journal of Law and Public Policy.* v. 14, nº 3, 1991, pp. 645–694.

Idem. Formalism. *The Yale Law Journal.* v. 97, n. 4, March 1988.

Idem. Easy Cases. *Modern Constitucional Theory: a Reader.* 5. ed. Org. John Garvey, Alexander Aleinikoff and Daniel Farber. São Paulo: West, 2004.

Idem. *Profiles, Probabilities and Stereotypes.* Cambridge: Harvard University Press, 2003.

SHEPPARD, Steve. The State Interest in the Good Citizen: Constitutional Balance Between the Citizen and the Perfectionist State. *Hastings Law Journal.* v. 45, n. 4, April 1994.

SCHEPERS, H. Heuristik. In: *Historisches Wörterbuch der Philosophie.* v. 3. Darmstadt: Wissenschaftliche Buchgesellschaft, 1974.

SIECKMANN, Jan-Reinard. *Regelmodelle und Prinzipien-modelle des Rechtssystems.* Baden-Baden: Nomos, 1990.

SILVA, Luis Virgílio Afonso da. O proporcional e o razoável. *Revista dos Tribunais.* v. 798. São Paulo: RT, 2002.

SOBOTA, Katharina. *Das Prinzip Rechtsstaat.* Tübingen: Mohr Siebeck, 1997.

SOMMERMANN, Karl-Peter. *Staatsziele und Staatszielbestimmungen.* Tübingen: Mohr Siebeck, 1997.

STEGMÜLLER, Wolfgang. *Hauptströmungen der Gegenwartsphilosophie.* 7th ed. v. 1. Stuttgart: Kröner, 1989.

STEINMETZ, Wilson Antônio. *Colisão de Direitos Fundamentais e o princípio da proporcionalidade.* Porto Alegre: Livraria do Advogado, 2001.

STEIN, Ernildo. Não podemos dizer a mesma coisa com outras palavras. *Miguel Reale: Estudos em homenagem a seus 90 anos.* Urbano Zilles (coord.). Porto Alegre: EDIPUCRS, 2000.

STELZER, Manfred. Das Wesensgehaltsargument und der Grundsatz der Verhältnismäßigkeit. Vienna: Springer, 1991.

STERN, Klaus. *Das Staatsrecht der Bundesrepublik Deutschland. Volumn I: Grundbegriffe und Grundlagen des Staatsrechts, Strukturprinzipien der Verfassung.* 2nd ed. Munich: Beck, 1984.

SUMMERS, Robert. Two Types of Substantive Reasons: The Core of a Theory of Common-Law Justification. *The Jurisprudence of Law's Form and Substance (Collected Essays in Law).* Aldershot: Ashgate, 2000. pp. 155–236.

TORRES, Ricardo Lobo. A legitimação dos Direitos Humanos e os Princípios da Ponderação e da Razoabilidade. In: *Legitimação dos Direitos Humanos.* Org. TORRES, Ricardo Lobo. Rio de Janeiro: Renovar, 2002.

TIPKE, Klaus. *Die Steuerrechtsordnung.* Volume I. Cologne: Otto Schmidt, 1993.

VARGA, Csaba. The Non-cognitive Character of the Judicial Establishment of Facts. In: *Praktische Vernunft und Rechtsanwendung. Archiv für Recht- und Sozialphilosophie*, v. 53, p. 232. Stuttgart: Franz Steiner, 1994.

VOGEL, Klaus/WALDHOFF, Christian. *Bonner Kommentar zum Grundgesetz*. 81st printing. 1997.

Idem. Christian. *Grundlagen des Finanzverfassungsrechts: Sonderausgabe des Bonner Kommentars zum Grundgesetz (Vorbemerkungen zu Art. 104a bis 115 GG)*. Heidelberg: Müller, 1999.

VOGEL, Klaus. *Wordwide vs. source of taxation of income - A review and re-evaluation of arguments*. International Tax Review (Org.), Fred C. de Hosson, Offprint from Intertax 8–11/1988.

WEINBERGER, Ota. *Rechtslogik*. 2nd ed. Berlin: Duncker und Humblot, 1989.

WITTGENSTEIN, Ludwig. *Tratado Lógico-Filosófico - Investigações Filosóficas*. Trad. M. S. Lourenço. Lisbon: Calouste Gulbenkian, 1981.

WRIGHT, Georg Henrik von. Sein und Sollen. In: *Normen, Werte und Handlungen*. Frankfurt am Main: Suhrkamp, 1994.

Idem. *Rationalität: Mittel und Zwecke*. In: Normen, Werte und Handlungen. Frankfurt am Main: Suhrkamp, 1994.

ZAGREBELSKY, Gustavo. Su ter aspetti della ragionevolleza. In: *Il principio di ragionevolezza nella giurisprudenza della Corte Costituzionale*. Milan: Giuffrè, 1994.

ZANCANER, Weida. Razoabilidade e moralidade: princípios concretizadores do perfil constitucional do Estado Social e Democrático de Direito. *Revista Diálogo Jurídico*, Salvador CAJ - Centro de Atualização Jurídica, ano I, nº 9, dezembro, 2001, p. 4. Available at <http://www.direitopublico.com.br>.

ZARADER, Marlene. *Heidegger et lês paroles de l'origine*. Paris: Librairie Philosophique J. VRIN, 1986.

NAME INDEX

SUBJECT INDEX

Law and Philosophy Library

1. E. Bulygin, J.-L. Gardies and I.Niiniluoto (eds.): *Man, Law and Modern Forms of Life.* With an Introduction by M.D. Bayles. 1985 ISBN 90-277-1869-5
2. W. Sadurski: *Giving Desert Its Due. Social Justice and Legal Theory. 1985* ISBN 90-277-1941-1
3. N. MacCormick and O. Weinberger: *An Institutional Theory of Law.* New Approaches to Legal Positivism. 1986 ISBN 90-277-2079-7
4. A. Aarnio: *The Rational as Reasonable.* A Treatise on Legal Justification. 1987 ISBN 90-277-2276-5
5. M.D. Bayles: *Principles of Law.* A Normative Analysis. 1987 ISBN 90-277-2412-1; Pb: 90-277-2413-X
6. A. Soeteman: *Logic in Law.* Remarks on Logic and Rationality in Normative Reasoning, Especially in Law. 1989 ISBN 0-7923-0042-4
7. C.T. Sistare: *Responsibility and Criminal Liability.* 1989 ISBN 0-7923-0396-2
8. A. Peczenik: *On Law and Reason.* 1989 ISBN 0-7923-0444-6
9. W. Sadurski: *Moral Pluralism and Legal Neutrality.* 1990 ISBN 0-7923-0565-5
10. M.D. Bayles: *Procedural Justice.* Allocating to Individuals. 1990 ISBN 0-7923-0567-1
11. P. Nerhot (ed.): *Law, Interpretation and Reality.* Essays in Epistemology, Hermeneutics and Jurisprudence. 1990 ISBN 0-7923-0593-0
12. A.W. Norrie: *Law, Ideology and Punishment.* Retrieval and Critique of the Liberal Ideal of Criminal Justice. 1991 ISBN 0-7923-1013-6
13. P. Nerhot (ed.): *Legal Knowledge and Analogy.* Fragments of Legal Epistemology, Hermeneutics and Linguistics. 1991 ISBN 0-7923-1065-9
14. O. Weinberger: *Law, Institution and Legal Politics.* Fundamental Problems of Legal Theory and Social Philosophy. 1991 ISBN 0-7923-1143-4
15. J. Wróblewski: *The Judicial Application of Law.* Edited by Z.Bańkowski and N. MacCormick. 1992 ISBN 0-7923-1569-3
16. T. Wilhelmsson: *Critical Studies in Private Law.* A Treatise on Need-Rational Principles in Modern Law. 1992 ISBN 0-7923-1659-2
17. M.D. Bayles: *Hart's Legal Philosophy.* An Examination. 1992 ISBN 0-7923-1981-8
18. D.W.P. Ruiter: *Institutional Legal Facts.* Legal Powers and their Effects. 1993 ISBN 0-7923-2441-2
19. J. Schonsheck: *On Criminalization.* An Essay in the Philosophy of the Criminal Law. 1994 ISBN 0-7923-2663-6
20. R.P. Malloy and J. Evensky (eds.): *Adam Smith and the Philosophy of Law and Economics.* 1994 ISBN 0-7923-2796-9
21. Z. Bańkowski, I. White and U. Hahn (eds.): *Informatics and the Foundations of Legal Reasoning.* 1995 ISBN 0-7923-3455-8
22. E. Lagerspetz: *The Opposite Mirrors.* An Essay on the Conventionalist Theory of Institutions. 1995 ISBN 0-7923-3325-X
23. M. van Hees: *Rights and Decisions.* Formal Models of Law and Liberalism. 1995 ISBN 0-7923-3754-9
24. B. Anderson: *"Discovery" in Legal Decision-Making.* 1996 ISBN 0-7923-3981-9
25. S. Urbina: *Reason, Democracy, Society.* A Study on the Basis of Legal Thinking. 1996 ISBN 0-7923-4262-3
26. E. Attwooll: *The Tapestry of the Law.* Scotland, Legal Culture and Legal Theory. 1997 ISBN 0-7923-4310-7

Law and Philosophy Library

27. J.C. Hage: *Reasoning with Rules.* An Essay on Legal Reasoning and Its Underlying Logic. 1997 ISBN 0-7923-4325-5
28. R.A. Hillman: *The Richness of Contract Law.* An Analysis and Critique of Contemporary Theories of Contract Law. 1997 ISBN 0-7923-4336-0; 0-7923-5063-4 (Pb)
29. C. Wellman: *An Approach to Rights.* Studies in the Philosophy of Law and Morals. 1997 ISBN 0-7923-4467-7
30. B. van Roermund: *Law, Narrative and Reality.* An Essay in Intercepting Politics. 1997 ISBN 0-7923-4621-1
31. I. Ward: *Kantianism, Postmodernism and Critical Legal Thought.* 1997 ISBN 0-7923-4745-5
32. H. Prakken: *Logical Tools for Modelling Legal Argument.* A Study of Defeasible Reasoning in Law. 1997 ISBN 0-7923-4776-5
33. T. May: *Autonomy, Authority and Moral Responsibility.* 1998 ISBN 0-7923-4851-6
34. M. Atienza and J.R. Manero: *A Theory of Legal Sentences.* 1998 ISBN 0-7923-4856-7
35. E.A. Christodoulidis: *Law and Reflexive Politics.* 1998 ISBN 0-7923-4954-7
36. L.M.M. Royakkers: *Extending Deontic Logic for the Formalisation of Legal Rules.* 1998 ISBN 0-7923-4982-2
37. J.J. Moreso: *Legal Indeterminacy and Constitutional Interpretation.* 1998 ISBN 0-7923-5156-8
38. W. Sadurski: *Freedom of Speech and Its Limits.* 1999 ISBN 0-7923-5523-7
39. J. Wolenski (ed.): *Kazimierz Opalek Selected Papers in Legal Philosophy.* 1999 ISBN 0-7923-5732-9
40. H.P. Visser 't Hooft: *Justice to Future Generations and the Environment.* 1999 ISBN 0-7923-5756-6
41. L.J. Wintgens (ed.): *The Law in Philosophical Perspectives.* My Philosophy of Law. 1999 ISBN 0-7923-5796-5
42. A.R. Lodder: *DiaLaw.* On Legal Justification and Dialogical Models of Argumentation. 1999 ISBN 0-7923-5830-9
43. C. Redondo: *Reasons for Action and the Law.* 1999 ISBN 0-7923-5912-7
44. M. Friedman, L. May, K. Parsons and J. Stiff (eds.): *Rights and Reason.* Essays in Honor of Carl Wellman. 2000 ISBN 0-7923-6198-9
45. G.C. Christie: *The Notion of an Ideal Audience in Legal Argument.* 2000 ISBN 0-7923-6283-7
46. R.S. Summers: *Essays in Legal Theory.* 2000 ISBN 0-7923-6367-1
47. M. van Hees: *Legal Reductionism and Freedom.* 2000 ISBN 0-7923-6491-0
48. R. Gargarella: *The Scepter of Reason.* Public Discussion and Political Radicalism in the Origins of Constitutionalism. 2000 ISBN 0-7923-6508-9
49. M. Iglesias Vila: *Facing Judicial Discretion.* Legal Knowledge and Right Answers Revisited. 2001 ISBN 0-7923-6778-2
50. M. Kiikeri: *Comparative Legal Reasoning and European Law.* 2001 ISBN 0-7923-6884-3
51. A.J. Menéndez: *Justifying Taxes.* Some Elements for a General Theory of Democratic Tax Law. 2001 ISBN 0-7923-7052-X
52. W.E. Conklin: *The Invisible Origins of Legal Positivism.* A Re-Reading of a Tradition. 2001 ISBN 0-7923-7101-1
53. Z. Bańkowski: *Living Lawfully.* Love in Law and Law in Love. 2001 ISBN 0-7923-7180-1

Law and Philosophy Library

54. A.N. Shytov: *Conscience and Love in Making Judicial Decisions.* 2001
ISBN 1-4020-0168-1
55. D.W.P. Ruiter: *Legal Institutions.* 2001 ISBN 1-4020-0186-X

Volumes 56–63 were published by Kluwer Law International.

---

56. G. den Hartogh: *Mutual Expectations.* A Conventionalist Theory of Law. 2002
ISBN 90-411-1796-2
57. W.L. Robison (ed.): *The Legal Essays of Michael Bayles.* 2002 ISBN 90-411-1835-7
58. U. Bindreiter: *Why Grundnorm?* A Treatise on the Implications of Kelsen's Doctrine. 2002 ISBN 90-411-1867-5
59. S. Urbina: *Legal Method and the Rule of Law.* 2002 ISBN 90-411-1870-5
60. M. Baurmann: *The Market of Virtue.* Morality and Commitment in a Liberal Society. 2002 ISBN 90-411-1874-8
61. G. Zanetti: *Political Friendship and the Good Life.* Two Liberal Arguments against Perfectionism. 2002 ISBN 90-411-1881-0
62. W. Sadurski (ed.): *Constitutional Justice, East and West.* 2002 ISBN 90-411-1883-7
63. S. Taekema: *The Concept of Ideals in Legal Theory.* 2003 ISBN 90-411-1971-X
64. J. Raitio: *The Principle of Legal Certainty in EC Law.* 2003 ISBN 1-4020-1217-9
65. E. Santoro: *Autonomy, Freedom and Rights.* A Critique of Liberal Subjectivity. 2003
ISBN 1-4020-1404-X
66. S. Eng: *Analysis of Dis/agreement – with particular reference to Law and Legal Theory.* 2003 ISBN 1-4020-1490-2
67. D. González Lagier: *The Paradoxes of Action.* (Human Action, Law and Philosophy). 2003 ISBN Hb-1-4020-1661-1
68. R. Zimmerling: *Influence and Power.* Variations on a Messy Theme. 2004
ISBN Hb-1-4020-2986-1
69. A. Stranieri and J. Zeleznikow (eds.): *Knowledge Discovery from Legal Databases.* 2005
ISBN 1-4020-3036-3
70. J. Hage: *Studies in Legal Logic.* 2005 ISBN 1-4020-3517-9
71. C. Wellman: *Medical Law and Moral Rights.* 2005 ISBN 1-4020-3751-1
72. T. Meisels: *Territorial Rights.* 2005 ISBN 1-4020-3822-4
73. G.W. Rainbolt: *The Concept of Rights.* 2005 ISBN 1-4020-3976-X
74. O. Ezra: *Moral Dilemmas in Real Life.* Current Issues in Applied Ethics. 2006
ISBN 1-4020-4103-9
75. N.T. Casals: *Group Rights as Human Rights.* A Liberal Approach to Multiculturalism. 2006 ISBN 1-4020-4208-6
76. C. Michelon Jr.: *Being Apart from Reasons.* The Role of Reasons in Public and Private Moral Decision-Making. 2006 ISBN 1-4020-4282-5
77. A.J. Menendez and E.O. Eriksen (eds): *Arguing Fundamental Rights.* 2006
ISBN 1-4020-4918-8
78. J. Stelmach and B. Brozek: *Methods of Legal Reasoning.* 2006 ISBN 1-4020-4936-6
79. M. La Torre: *Constitutionalism and Legal Reasoning.* 2006 ISBN 1-4020-5594-3
80. P. Costa and D. Zolo (eds): *The rule of Law.* History, Theory and Criticism. 2007
ISBN 978-1-4020-5744-1
81. H. Avila: *Theory of Legal Principles.* 2007 ISBN 978-1-4020-5878-3

GPSR Compliance

The European Union's (EU) General Product Safety Regulation (GPSR) is a set of rules that requires consumer products to be safe and our obligations to ensure this.

If you have any concerns about our products, you can contact us on ProductSafety@springernature.com

In case Publisher is established outside the EU, the EU authorized representative is:

Springer Nature Customer Service Center GmbH
Europaplatz 3
69115 Heidelberg, Germany

Batch number: 10755292

Printed by Printforce, the Netherlands